You can't see V
Living with Cluste

Original Title

SCHMERZ FRISST SEELE
Leben mit Clusterkopfschmerzen
158 pages / 11,80 EUR (D)

© Pomaska-Brand Verlag

All rights to distribution, including excerpts, within the German-speaking world reserved

Cover designs:
Rafael Häusler

All rights reserved, especially the right to manual, electronic, or photographic duplication, storage and processing in computer systems, printing in newspapers or publications.

Translated by Thorin Engeseth in Summer 2017

Very special thanks to M.G.
Without his commitment this version might not have existed.

Writing means to read oneself.
Max Frisch

Good memories can save your life.
Film quote «The Punisher»

Important Note

The trade names of medicines are not the same throughout the world.

For example: Imigran is called Imitrex in several other countries.

I used the trade names from Germany. Cause the eBook is available worldwide, there is no chance to translate this in way which is valid everywhere. Therefore, I remain with the original names.

Introduction	9
After the book is before the book	11
Instead of a Foreword	14
Definition	17
What is Cluster Headache?	19
Who am I?	22
Biography	27
Before the Diagnosis	29
After the Diagnosis	33
Questions	37
Why Me?	39
Religion	40
The Lord	42
The Question of Condition	44
Two-Class Society	46
Quo Vadis?	49
Relationship Issues	57
Perspectives	61
More than Pain	63
15 Minutes	69
Headache	71
Turmoil	72
Self-Harm	74
How Does It Feel The Morning After?	75
Over?	76
Answers	80
Logistics of a Chronic Illness	82
Headache Journal	83
Severe Disability	86
I'm Getting by, Right?	88
Enjoy Life	90
Velosophy	94
Outlooks	98
Miscellaneous	101
Hard Drive Receiver	103
Rusted End Caps	103
Rehabilitation or not?	104

- Yoga 105
- Doctor Visits are a Form of Social Contact 106
- Traditional Chinese Medicine (TCM), Homeopathy, Shamanism, Etc. 106
- Holding On 107
- Traumatisation 107
- Smoking 109
- Time 109
- Minimising Irritants 109
- FAQ - Frequently Asked Questions 110

Appendix 123
- Conclusion in Key Points 125
- Contacts / Internet Addresses 126
- Acknowledgments 128
- Epilogue 129
- About the Author 131

Supplementary Texts 133
- What Happened? 135
- Thanks 136
- Education in Hamburg 138
- Bochum Cluster Headache Day 2015 141
- From the Headache News 01/2015 146
- On Creaking, Crunching, and Clicking 150
- A Journey into the Fundamental Research of Migraine 152
- The Right Diagnosis? 155
- Paths to Information 157
- My Booboo is Bigger than Yours 159
- Get-well Wishes 162
- A Look to Our Neighbours – What is the Significance of Migraine 163
- Botox in the Pterygopalatine Ganglion 165
- How do you deal with depressed thoughts? 166
- Migraine and Nitrates 168
- Fear, Part 1 169
- Fear, Part 2 171
- Diagnosis is Simple – Treatment is Not 175
- Well-Intentioned – Accessibility 177

Fear Part 3, on the Path to Inspiration & Motivation............ 179
Bochum Cluster Headache Patient Day 2017........................ 182
On Accepting Lactose Intolerance... 187
From wood to branch 191
The very last page 194

Introduction

According to one fairly prevalent myth, the Eskimos have a hundred different words for snow. This is actually a tall tale that originated in 1911 with the German linguist, ethnologist, and anthropologist Franz Boas, and it formed from a lack of understanding of the polysynthetic language spoken by Northern peoples. Only in 1986 did anthropologist Laura Martin write an article titled "Eskimo Words for Snow" in American Anthropologist, in which she clarified this myth. Franz Boas had probably only wished to express that the Eskimos had adjusted their language to suit their environment. Someone surrounded by snow will have a more nuanced way of describing it.

Just like the inhabitants of the North Pole know snow, I know different types of headache. Each one has to be addressed differently. The traditional terms for affective (e.g. nagging, agonizing, paralyzing, terrible, severe) and sensory (e.g. pulsating, throbbing, stabbing, dull, pressing, burning) descriptions of pain are not nearly sufficient to comprehensively describe the overall artwork that is cluster headache.

Pain is that which one perceives as such. Suffering from pain can make it incredibly difficult for one to communicate with their environment. Pain is a highly subjective perception. It is difficult to comprehensibly and clearly explain it to other people.

This book documents and describes the effects of a chronic illness, cluster headache, on my life, thoughts, and worldview. I am afflicted, making me a patient and not a doctor. I cannot and do not want to make any diagnoses. Rather, I want to try to put the pain I have endured - and its consequences - down on paper. It's also sort of like I'm explaining to a Majorcan the difference between snow, firn, crusted snow, and corn snow.

When I decided to write down the story of my illness, I was far more bitter than I am now. I've since become mortified by my original ideas for a title, namely: "No Escape - I'd Sell My Soul to Get Rid of the Pain", "The Pain Stays with You", "You Have the Pain", "You Can't Share Suffering", "Nobody Can Help You - You Have to Live with the Ache", and even "Cluster Headache - When You Torture Yourself". I tried to scream the ache away, because nowhere did I feel like I was sufficiently understood. Thankfully I have since opened up my ears, and ultimately learned how to listen to myself.

After the book is before the book

Thoughts and Facts for the Second Edition.

What actually happens when you want to use a book like this one to give the entire world deep, or maybe the deepest, insight into your soul? When you lay out all of your flaws and shortcomings out on a silver platter? When you pull your trousers down and stand naked in the wind?
When I wrote the first sentences down years ago, all I wanted to do was scream out - well, describe - my pain. To cry out everything under the sun because nobody could help me and nobody had listened. I was miserable.
While the book was being made I actually never thought that I was performing a public striptease in doing so. It was clear to me what I was doing, but I had never considered that side of it before. Another author pointed it out to me on the first day of the book launch. "When strangers get into bed with you, or rather your book."
Yes, it's possible. Some of my most intimate thoughts are lying on the nightstands of complete strangers in the form of this book. Yet over the course of many therapy sessions and conversations I had already learned that outward expression is important. Your thoughts and feelings can only be perceived by others if they are expressed. I either want somebody to understand how I'm doing, or I don't. I wanted it!
Now, I'm not happy that it is the way it is, but I'm also not embarrassed. There's nothing at all to be nervous about.
Or is there?
Of course there is!
Because I didn't know how the outside world would react to what I have experienced, thought, and written down. People close to me, people who already know me, had read it. Many publishers had read excerpts of it, but most

of them didn't see the manuscript turning into a book. Now everyone can read it.

Some have already done it, and in turn I've heard echoes back from them. People I knew in passing. People I've known for a long time but who did not know this side of me. People who knew me before I got sick. And, of course, people who didn't know me at all but who suffer from the same disease. The reception from all of them has been entirely positive. It's exactly the type of understanding I have always hoped for. Moreover, other sufferers said that they could identify with at least a few aspects. This is where I achieved my goal.

I am happy

It's how I know I didn't produce a pile of crap. All reception from here on out is a bonus. Hopes will now be fulfilled. I have also been told that my ideas are accepted and that people can learn from my own journey. I hear this even from people who don't suffer from cluster headache whatsoever. They have read this book and let me know that they have been able to benefit from it. Inside I had already long suspected that many of my strategies for managing cluster headache could also be used for similar (e.g. migraine) or completely different diseases. Going even one step further than I had hoped fills me with a little pride.

At the very least I did everything right in turning my deepest thoughts outward. I have only benefited from it.

The book has also benefited, especially from its readers. Obviously I alone did not think of all of the relevant questions and issues. I respond to a selection of the most important and common questions in the FAQ chapter. In it I don't provide any general advice, but rather disclose my own views, convictions, and the processes that have proven helpful to me. I cannot predict which actions will be the right ones for everyone. Everybody is different, and everybody has to find their own way. But learning from something and being inspired by it is not only allowed, but desired and encouraged.

Another victory for me is when I come across my own conclusions in a similar form in other books or presentations. In A Journey of 1000 Miles Begins with a Single Step, Luise Reddemann writes about stopping to think, as there is no silver bullet and everyone has to work on paving their own way.

Last year during one of his presentations, Dr. Hartmut Göbel spoke quite impressively about how headache patients often possess a mind that absorbs a lot of - perhaps too much - sensory input. The key phrase was "minimisation of irritants". Such overlap with my own experiences solidifies my certainty that I am headed in the right direction, doing what I like to do and looking contentedly toward the future. This is true even when I wake up in a bad mood after a night marred by three attacks, because I admittedly not free from this demon. This book is about living with a disease, not conquering it.

As the cherry on top, my attending neurologist spontaneously wrote me a foreword. She attests that the title of the book is wrong because the pain has certainly not eaten my soul, but at the very worst has gnawed at it, and I take that to be great praise to be put up on my shelf. No, I'll frame it and hang it up on the wall. But I must also return it, because she is not entirely innocent in this matter. When I first sat in her waiting room my soul was nearly gone. What began with a smiley - drawn by Mrs. Gendolla on a pack of medication - turned into a relationship of trust that I cannot imagine being more wonderful.

Instead of a Foreword

You'll Never Walk Alone
by Dr. Astrid Gendolla

I have been a practicing physician in Essen, Germany for twenty years now, and in this time I have worked with so many headache patients that I lost count. I most frequently encounter people with migraines who no longer know where to go about their terrible pain. The most insidious, however, is cluster headache. It manifests in attacks, and comes virtually out of nowhere. Attacks entail extremely severe pain that can last for a long time, and then vanish just as suddenly. The dreadful thing about this disease is the absolute powerlessness against its randomness. Attacks can return at any time, without warning, without abstention. People who live with this disease are simultaneously living in constant fear.
Rafael Häusler has faced this fear. He meticulously describes the stages of the disease, reflects on his life with cluster headache, and tries to find answers. But there is one thing that I would like to firmly disagree with Rafael Häusler on. The title of the book does not apply, at least to the author himself. The pain has not eaten his soul, and as his attending physician I can confirm this. Perhaps it has tried to, perhaps it has gnawed at his soul from time to time. But Rafael Häusler defied it. I am certain that his journey must have been difficult, the road bumpy, but ultimately so successful that he is able to write about all of his experiences. A beneficial process? It is not my place to say. In any case writing is a known way to look at the entirety of a given subject. Rafael Häusler's notes, turned into a book, also have another effect: they help other people better understand the disease and those who suffer from it, and they show other patients one very important message: "You'll Never Walk Alone". There are people

who understand you, who feel what you feel, who are with you. That alone makes this book invaluable.

I am happy and grateful that my profession allows me to join Rafael Häusler on this journey, and to speak with him on a regular basis. I can truly recommend this book to you from the bottom of my heart.

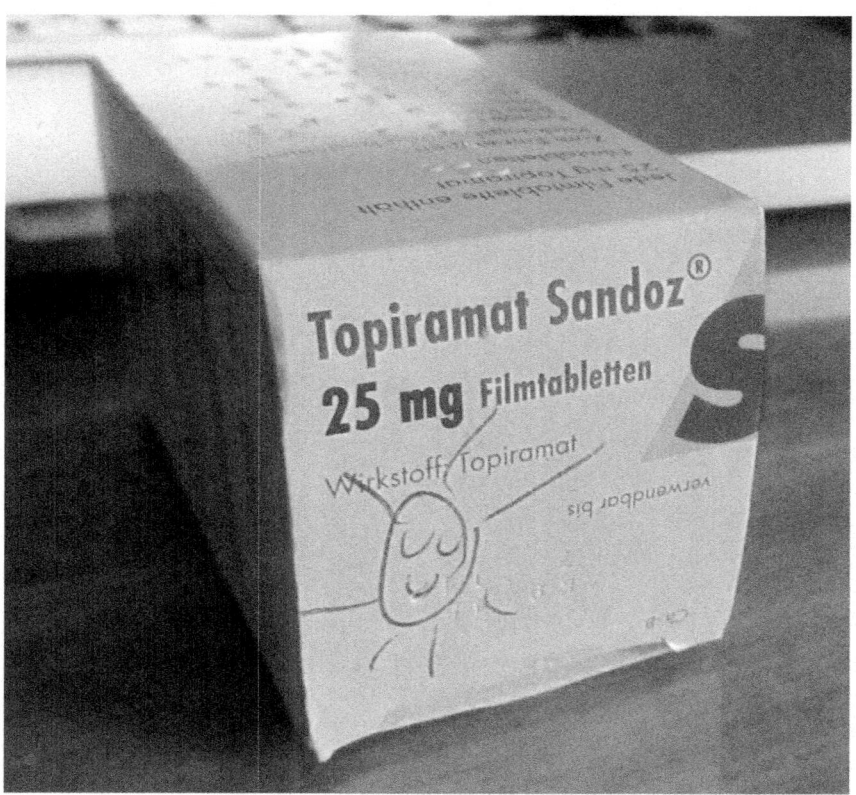

Definition

A definition of the symptoms of cluster headache syndrome. This also includes a personal introduction, along with the description of my own symptoms.

"It is better to light a candle than to curse the darkness."
Chinese proverb

What is Cluster Headache?

The phenomenon of cluster headache has been re-described a number of times over the years, the result being many names for this rather rare sickness. In accordance with ICD-10, medical professionals refer to cluster headache with the shorthand code G44.0.
The ICD-10 from 11 is the current version of a globally recognised diagnosis classification and encryption system issued by the World Health Organisation (WHO).
Former terms and designations include:
Ciliary neuralgia, erythromelalgia of the head, erythroprosopalgia, hemicrania angioparalytica, hemicrania periodica neuralgiformis, histaminic, (Bing-)Horton syndrome, Harris-Horton syndrome, Harris's migrainous neuralgia, Gardner's petrosus neuralgia, Sluder's neuralgia, neuralgia of the Ganglion sphenopalatinum, and Vidian neuralgia.
Another common term - "suicide headache" - has understandably fallen out of fashion.

An unbelievable number of names for a disease with just as many facets. It remains a mystery why there have been so many ways to refer to a relatively rare illness in the last 150 years. It could be because, truthfully, no two cluster headaches are alike. Yet it gives utterance to the helplessness against the phenomenon.
Cluster headache, properly known as cluster headache syndrome (CHS), is a chronic and untreatable disease. It is one of the trigeminal autonomic cephalalgia (TACs), which also include paroxysmal hemicrania (PH) and SUNCT syndrome (short-lasting unilateral neuralgiform headache with conjunctival injection and tearing).
Wikipedia defines TACs as follows:
"Trigeminal autonomic cephalalgia is the name for a type of primary headache that occurs with pain on one side of the head in the trigeminal nerve area and symptoms in

autonomic systems on the same side, such as eye watering and redness or drooping eyelids."

The term "trigeminal autonomic cephalalgia" was first used in 1997 by Peter J. Goadsby and Richard B. Lipton.

Other similar headaches include hemicrania continua (which entails constant pain but the autonomic characteristics are less constant), and SUNA syndrome (short-lasting unilateral neuralgiform headache attacks with cranial autonomic symptoms). However, these are categorised as "Other primary headaches" in the headache classification of the International Headache Society (IHS).

The various types of trigeminal autonomic headaches primarily differ by the time patterns - duration and frequency - of the attacks.

The signs are extremely severe (head) pain attacks. Relatively distinct characteristics of CHS are the unilateral occurrence and distinct accompanying symptoms like reddened and watery eyes, swollen nasal mucosa, contraction of the pupils, and sweating from the face. The pain lasts for 15 to 180 minutes. The number of attacks varies greatly from one person's cluster headache to the next. They could be nighttime attacks every two days, or multiple throughout the day. My personal maximum is five attacks per day. Contrary to all other types of headache, a cluster attack entails unrest. And much unlike migraines, there is no sensitivity to light and noise.

The intensity of the pain can easily lead to unconsciousness. During a severe attack the sufferer may not be responsive, and could not be physically able to use the muscles required to tie their shoelaces.

CHS is divided into episodic and chronic manifestations, whereby the episodic manifestation is also a chronic disease. With episodic cluster headache, the pain attacks occur frequently within a certain period of time and are broken up by temporary, symptom-free phases of remission. The pain episode can last from a few weeks to a number of months. The remission phases can even span years. If there are no such remission phases, or if they are too short to provide any actual respite, this is referred to as chronic cluster headache.

Ironically, cluster headache is not dangerous, despite the intense pain. The medical world sometimes refers to it as benign suffering, as it is not fatal like some diseases, e.g. cancer. Thank you, dear medical professionals, for this trivialisation.

The extent to which CHS affects one's personal life depends on the number and frequency of the attacks. If someone experiences two months of episodes per year with nightly attacks every other day, and enjoys ten-month remission phases in between, they will probably be asked from time to time why they look so unrested. But if someone suffers from the chronic manifestation and experiences an average of three or more high-intensity attacks every day, a normal life is most likely no longer conceivable. Instead cluster headache becomes a constant companion that engrains itself in every aspect of one's life. Especially with severe manifestations, the level of impact also highly depends on the sufferer's social environment and financial security.

For me the pain is not just a phenomenon that comes and goes. Indeed, it is clear to me that the pain is just made up of electrical signals - nerve impulses - running amok in my brain. But I feel the pain, or pains, to be a lifelong companion. It's just like a living creature. Cluster headache is a raging animal mercilessly striking at me with no pattern, no warning. A migraine, on the other hand, is like a jealous creature. It wants all of the attention for itself, but is fair enough to announce its arrival in advance.

Further information, especially concerning the current treatment recommendations of cluster headache, can be found in the current guidelines of the German Neurology Society, among other places. These guidelines can be found online at: http://www.dgn.org/leitlinien.html

Who am I?

My Personal Cluster Headache

As of the time at which this book is being conceived in my head, I am a male individual born 38 years ago in Germany's Ruhr region, and I still live here.
Cluster headache has been a part of my life for more than ten years now. In this time it has become more and more integrated into my life and continues to take control. The course of my life was certainly not shaped by it alone, but it definitely played a significant role.
Much of the information in this book gradually came together in the form of journal entries and originally served to process what I have experienced. On top of that are insights and strategies that I have worked out over the years and which have been imparted to me. If my experiences can help even just one other person affected by cluster headache, then this book has been worth it.
Another reason for writing was that I have never been able to explain to someone everything that's written herein.
This book took three years to create, and in that time I participated in a number of different measures and conducted a variety of treatments. This absolutely difficult therapeutic work in particular gave me new perspectives that I had ceased to believe in, despite my sickness.
It is easy to say that a person is no more than what pain has made them into, or even what is left of them as a result. But only I can decide how much I permit such self-abandonment. It's my inner attitude that give me a certain degree of control over my well-being. This attitude can either be a life-destroying downward spiral or a reliable source of support in threatening internal and external situations, depending on one's mood. The desire to actively participate in one's own development is absolutely necessary to break through what could become a vicious cycle.

My own personal cluster headache can be characterized as follows:
- Affected side: right
- Occurring since 1999
- Diagnosed in late 2004
- Up to five attacks per day (raised this to eight a day in February 2016)
- Attack duration: 15 to 120 minutes
- Pain intensity as bad as unconsciousness, not responsive, impaired motor skills
- Originally about three months of episodes and nine months of remission per year. Eventually much longer episodes
- Accompanying systems like watery eyes and runny/congested nose not particularly distinct

Of course, the primary symptom is and remains the pain. Its long-term recurrence results in other symptoms as well. I define the following symptoms as primary side-effects:

- Sleep disorders
- Concentration disorders
- Amnesic aphasia
- Paranoia when falling asleep
- Brief stinging pains (1 – 5 minutes)
- Loss of libido (over a span of months)

I consider some other side-effects to be secondary:

- Depression (BDI-II 43 points, depression starting at 30)
- Impairment of physical performance (worst-case scenario with Topamax. I had to look at a packet to remember what the tablets are even called - forgetfulness)

- Impairment of mental performance
- States of anxiety/panic (e.g. if no medication is within reach)
- Alternation between aggression and apathy – very hard for relatives and friends to deal with
- Auto-aggression/tendency toward self-harm
- Extreme forgetfulness
- Listlessness/no motivation
- Lethargy/sluggishness
- Sweating attacks and other vegetative disorders. These do not always precede/follow pain attacks.

What else does my cluster headache do to me:

Photosensitivity

It has made me sensitive to light, especially with regard to light reflexes. It is thus not possible for me to spend time outdoors unprotected from the sun from April to October. Otherwise I would experience severe, migraine-like headaches and nausea within a very short period (< 5 minutes). As a result I can generally only go outdoors with a hat and sunglasses, especially when it's really warm out. Even when I'm doing somewhat better, I can only go outside with "protective clothing". It's entirely unknown why that is, and it is an incredible impediment to my everyday life.

Weight gain

The many medications I have taken caused me to gain weight. Yet the reward principle (chocolate after nightly pain attacks) and subsequent irregular meals on the days after attacks also played a part.

Mobility

It feels like I have aged 30 years, as all of my bones ache. Of those 30, 10 to 15 are certainly because of Topamax. Without Topamax I do much better, but still not good. To give a specific example, it is impossible for me to go up a set of stairs right after waking up.

Attacks after moments of strain

Pain attacks really like setting in after or during physical strain - e.g. riding my bike for 30 to 60 minutes. If nothing happens then, nothing will happen later. But this is not always the case, and happens about half the time. I get the impression that the symptoms start in brief phases of recovery, e.g. when I'm cruising down a mountain. What gives me this impression? Not much, aside from the fact that I can now only engage in my favorite hobby for a limited amount of time.

You can visualize someone suffering from pain by comparing them to a car in the winter. The pain behaves like frost. Only when it's cold enough will the car's motor fail, as the battery is no longer delivering enough power to rotate the starter. This image also illustrates another situation that I find myself in. The line between being able and unable to work is not fluid, but is hard and abrupt. If the pain exceeds a certain level, I sink backward into my condition and all corresponding symptoms promptly worsen.
Then when the car just starts up again, the heating works and it drives as through it had a fresh, fully charged battery. If I forget to repair my empty battery the car may break down again the next day. If I accidentally leave the light on, it definitely will.
But contrary to cars, which can be replaced with a bus, train, or taxi in an emergency, there is no replacement for one's own body. That's why it's important for me to know the limit in time.

Biography

How my life looked before the disease, what remains of it as the attacks grew in frequency. And how I lost my courage, and a few other things.

"Over time the soul becomes dyed with the colour of its thoughts."
Marcus Aurelius

Before the Diagnosis

Headaches have never been a stranger to me. My mother had migraines now and then, so it was normal for me to have the occasional headache. But shortly before the turn of the millennium, I experienced an entirely new type of pain.
I cannot pinpoint the exact date of my first cluster attack, as I did not record any precise information in the first years. In the first one or two years, though, it was notable and distinctive that the attacks only occurred at night. Over a span of about two months I was torn out of sleep in this harsh manner more frequently. It felt like something was smouldering in my head. Always in the same spot. So I would wander through my flat, crumple up on the floor, press my pulsating and burning temple against cool objects in an attempt to alleviate the pain. Every night it took one or two hours for the pain to subside.
I tried all of the commonly available swallowable, chewable, or effervescent painkillers to find the fastest possible combination. And I always wondered why the tablets worked quickly sometimes, slowly other times, and other times not at all. Now I know that they never worked. Every now and then I was just lucky that the attack was just over in half an hour or so.
My general practitioner, whom I first approached with the matter, had no idea where my pain could be coming from. He prescribed stronger tablets, which of course did not help either. At the time I always had a faint impression that the pain was coming from my upper jaw. I remembered a root canal operation. But the dentist also could not find any issues. The X-ray showed a slight shadow on a root in my upper jaw. In my desperation I asked that the healthy tooth be extracted, in the hopes that it was the culprit. Of course, it wasn't. My desperation intensified.
But before I could subject my body to any more nonsense, the episode was over and I ceased to exhibit any

symptoms for a number of months. The gap in my teeth, which still serves as a daily reminder of those times, still bothers me. But I was happy that this phantom pain was finally gone.

I would have happily left the pain behind me. But when the next episode started up, the pain did not only occur at night, but during the day as well. Now the pain had found a home behind my right eye, and no longer seemed to be coming from my jaw. I ingested painkillers like Smarties, and started to become withdrawn. Nothing is fun anymore when you have headaches. The waves of pain were so intense during the day that I was unable to do anything while they were happening.

Problems at work and in my personal life were amplified. The idea that the pain was from a tumour started to marinate in my head. There had to be a reason for this monstrous pain. The image of a foreign body in my head, no smaller than a chicken egg, formed before my mind's eye. Yet magnetic resonance imaging (an MRI) did not find anything. None of the doctors had any idea what I could be missing. Every test returned with one result: I am healthy.

That still did nothing to stop the constantly recurring pains that were driving me to insanity. I consoled myself by saying, "It's just pain, it won't kill you, it just hurts." This attitude actually helped me a little - just not a lot. Now I know that this approach was entirely sensible and can be seen as cognitive behavioural therapy.

With every passing day marred by this pain, it became less clear to me why I was even living and what my purpose was. Death increasingly became a sensible alternative. Naturally, my professional and personal life suffered. I became newly single, and then newly unemployed.

A cycle begins at this point. During the pain episode, all motivation collapses. The cluster wrings me out and shatters me against the wall. Once I'm lying in shards on the ground, it subsides. Sometimes it's more difficult to maintain a normal life after that, to sweep all your pieces back up and reorganise yourself - all just to ensure your own survival. However, such euphoric ideas like quality of living and optimism remain alien to me. I am no longer alive, I merely exist.

In late 2004 I was deep in the middle of a pain episode, lost all of my motivation once more, and only had a tattered life to look back on. But this time, a few simple, small things led to drastic changes.
One night in the first or second week of December I was sitting in front of my computer and asked the internet, "What if constant headaches make me unable to work?" Specifically, I enter the words "headaches" and "unable to work". When I saw what this simple question returned to me, it was as though the Oracle of Delphi had just paid me a personal visit. The resulting keyword was "cluster headache", and there were pages with personal stories and pages of clinics who provided a definition and description. The greatest wealth of information can be found on www.clusterkopf.de, the websites of the CSG e.V. (or, to provide its full name, the Federal Association of Self-Help Groups for Cluster Headache Patients and Their Loved Ones).
In all of the stories, reports from sufferers, and the forum posts that I read that night, I found a lot of things that I must have experienced in the past years. Suddenly I was certain that I had at least found the name for my invisible, overpowering opponent.
There are not many self-help groups in Germany. Thankfully I live in a megalopolis, and a self-help group met in the next city over. The next meeting was even in a few days. With my newly acquired knowledge, and thanks to the lists of doctors on the info pages, I finally found a doctor who might be able to help me. And I greedily learned that there is medication that can provide relief. This information was like rain the desert for me.
At the next meeting of the self-help group I was given further confirmation that my assumption was correct. Two

days later I was visiting the doctor I had picked and everything was clear in just a few minutes. The suffering I had endured over the past five years was compressed into one diagnosis: cluster headache. Armed with prescriptions for Imigran and oxygen, I was on my way home. Now I finally had weapons against my nemesis that, just a few days before, did not even have a name.

After the Diagnosis

It is abundantly clear to anyone who can no longer walk because of an accident or an illness that they rely on assistance in the form of a wheelchair. Someone who becomes blind will not have any illusions that they will be able to lead the same life they had up until that point. After the firm diagnosis of "cluster headache", however, it took a while for me to accept that it was now, and would remain, a part of my life.
But knowing that I suffer from cluster headache did not mean that I had found the off-switch. It also did not mean that I would perform Step A, take Medication B, and then be able to lead a pain-free life overnight.
For me cluster headache had been a loyal companion for years, a part of my life. But now it had a name, a face. That does not make it disappear, but rather more tangible. I was given prescriptions for every recommended standard medication, and was allowed to experiment to figure out what worked best for me.
Over the years I tried different means and methods for prophylaxis and acute treatment. Not everything worked, but thankfully some did. Cortisone pulse therapies had no effect on me. In terms of prophylaxis, Topamax only had dramatic side-effects, and Imigran Nasal left an absolutely ghastly taste in my throat. All of the triptans administered in tablet form were fruitless.
It became apparent over time that the first-choice medications from the guidelines of the German Neurological Society (GNS) for treating cluster headache and trigeminal autonomic cephalalgias were actually the best choice for me as well. This entailed high to very high doses of Verapamil for prophylaxis. At least 720 mg per day proved effective in my case. However, after 480 mg the side-effects of Verapamil were so strong that I had to overcome a lot just to take a higher dosage. However, the pain relief that came as a result was absolutely worth it.

I successfully took oxygen, which has to be inhaled with a high power density, to acutely curtail the attacks. 12 to 15 litres per minute are absolutely necessary, but the inhalation of oxygen only alleviates and shortens the attacks. A cluster headache attack can actually be eliminated with a subcutaneous injection of Imigran. The shot takes effect within five minutes and actually gets rid of the pain. The day I first took a shot of Imigran will be a special anniversary for the rest of my days.

It was the evening of 16 December 2004, when the very first season of the television show *TV Total's* high diving competition event Turmspringen was airing. It felt like an inner fire was tearing through all of my veins to the tips of my extremities. After a few minutes it felt like all of the droning in my head vanished in a single breath. I lifted my head and looked around, confused. The pain was gone. The pain that had caused me to writhe on the floor for so many hours, that left me powerless and which was responsible for so many restless nights. Click - it was turned off! I sat alone on the old furniture in my poorly heated flat and, in that moment, I felt simply unbeatable.

The 0.5 ml injection solution, which contains 6 mg of the agent sumatriptan, can have life-changing effects. To this day it is downright euphoric to take an Imigran injection - especially after a long break - and to feel (in the truest sense of the word) the medication in your veins and to just be able to get rid of the pain so easily.

Yet for as clear as it seems, it has many side-effects. I learned this as I started regularly taking too much of it. In my case, "too much" was about ten injections per week. So not during every attack. As a result I wound up in such a state that I felt like I was in the middle of a giant cotton ball. I didn't care about anything, and I did not pay anything any mind. A friend asked what was wrong, and said I looked really dazed. I am still unable to find a better way to describe the way I felt at the time.

Of course I learned that, at the time, I was no longer able to responsibly operate a motor vehicle. I could no longer (or rather, should no longer) drive a car. Everything simply happens too fast out on the road. Thankfully it only took a few close calls to bring me to this conclusion.

There is another memory that burned itself into my brain: I stored letters on my kitchen table for three months. The post piled up. I was horrified, and it proved to me that I still had a lot to learn in order to better live with my disease.

Zomig Nasal joined the medication duo of oxygen and Imigran Inject in 2010. Zomig Nasal is also a triptan with the more recent agent zolmitriptan. Like the injection form of sumatriptan, zolmitriptan as a nasal spray has been approved to treat cluster headache. While Zomig Nasal also leaves an undesirable taste in the throat, it's not as long-lasting and stubborn as Imigran Nasal's aftertaste. In my experience its effects are not as absolutely certain, and it doesn't always work. But when it does, it promises twelve pain-free hours. This makes it life-changing.

Ultimately, I have found fortune in misfortune! I attest to oxygen, and the two medications approved to treat cluster headache - Imigran and Zomig - work as well.

Questions

A number of questions I have asked myself and which have long gone unanswered. It took many discussions with other sufferers to learn that I was not the only one asking them.

We rarely think about what we have, but always about what we don't.
Arthur Schopenhauer

Why Me?

Why is this happening to me? Why now? This question can arise any time someone reaches a difficult time in their life, and clusterheads aren't the only ones who ask it. Some people ask it over and over again.
I don't know the answer to it, and the fruitless search is tiring. As a result, the question ultimately only amplifies the exhaustion. But circumstances prevent one from actually putting it out of their mind.
I have lived with cluster headache for a good decade now. In that time there have been good days and bad. The pain doesn't care what type of day it is when it sets in. Wildly erratic, it has not followed any specific rhythm for years now. I am entirely certain that it has completely disconnected from any inner and outer influences. It appears as though it has its own mind, as though it were its own entity. It shows up and dominates whenever it deems fit.
Why me? When it comes to migraines in particular, we look for its cause in an imbalance of the soul, its needs or its demands. It actually seems that such a connection can be found in most migraine cases. In his comprehensive book about migraines, Oliver Sacks writes that there is a reason behind every migraine. He reached this conclusion after investigating more than 1,000 cases.
Yet cluster headache is not a type of migraine, but rather a disease that may be related. So, dear doctors, do not treat cluster headache as though it were a form of migraine, even if there are unquestionable parallels between them. In my own head I know four different types of headache, and each of them wants to be treated differently. Each demands its own personal reaction.
"Why me?" is a question that may never have an answer, but we still have the potential to make sure that cluster headache is recognised as an actual, independent disease. We don't just have a headache, and we don't have a type of migraine.

Religion

Cluster headache is brutal. It strikes its innocent victim without warning. It's human nature to seek an explanation in religion when rationality cannot provide any.
Why does suffer from cluster headache at all? Why do they exhibit these painful attacks? Physicians differentiate between circadian (daily) and circannual (annual) rhythms. It is certainly not the only, and absolutely not the largest, unsolved puzzle in this world, but for those affected it is by far the most interesting.
In such cases many people, at least in Western Europe, are conditioned to turn to divine counsel as a universal explanation for the unexplainable. Indeed it provides tremendous relief when one is able to simply believe in a higher power in this situation.
In his book Angels & Demons, Dan Brown writes the protagonist Robert Langdon as saying, "Faith is a gift that I have yet to receive." And in his book The Happiness Code (Der Glückscode), the author Dieter Broers - whom I believe to be firmly rooted in the abyss of the esoteric - writes, "The Bible knows that faith can move mountains. Without wanting to compete with the Book of all books, I would like to add one thing: thought can create mountains."
Actually, with each attack the sufferer finds themselves facing the why-me question again. At some point I also began thinking in that direction. Always "why me?". Is it some kind of punishment? It was one claimed in jest that if things aren't going right in life, it must be because of exorbitant misconduct in a past life. So I lose karma points because I used to be a rowing drummer on the Rome-Carthage row galley?
To be honest, there has been a moral transgression in my life that I committed before my cluster headache began. To be prosaic, this transgression also wasn't really that bad. Given a hypothetical proportionality, half of humanity would suffer from headaches in this case, and a not-so-

insignificant portion of the population would go up in flames.
I'm not very receptive to esoteric and theological ideas as a matter of principle. In times of weakness, when my brain convulsions have been laying on the grill of pain for too long and too often, I've still sought out those ideas regardless. Whenever the pain subsides a little, the same questions always come back to me: "Why me?", "Why is this happening to me?", and "What am I being punished for?"

Today I know that these questions don't bring anyone a step further. Acceptance and tolerance are the key words. Still, it's not pretty and it's not fun. But nobody ever said it was.
Should I ever again lean toward faith in a higher power or anything God-given instead of naked fate, I will save myself by remembering that God is not infallible, and its ground crew especially aren't.
Marianne Thomas made this same point quite wonderfully during a radio special on Émilie du Châtelet on SWR 2. Émilie du Châtelet and Voltaire subjected the Bible to a thorough analysis and drafted a critical commentary. And because she loves logical reasoning, she addresses the story of the creation with distinct irony: "How amusing that the first three days were marked by night and morning before the sun was even created on the fourth."

The Lord

In 2009 I participated in a rehabilitation programme in Bad Wildungen, in the north of the state of Hessen. While conversing during the psychological consultation, the psychologist at the on-site clinic suggested that I give my pain a name and a shape in order to turn it into a person. Then I should reveal everything from this person's perspective - the entire story from the pain's point of view.
I then envisioned a figure similar to the god Thor. I had never intensely researched Germanic or Nordic mythology, so this was a purely intuitive name. The figure of a sovereign lord, the God of Thunder. It was he who does not suffer anybody beside him, whose power outshines everything, who darkens the sun, or who is the sun itself in which one burns and dies out.
He's not some good lord who is well-disposed toward his people. He is merciless, even sadistic. He lets his host bleed until they are down on their knees, limply following every command. So the lord, who, in the grander scheme of things, is really only there for a short period, is still always present. Omnipresent. He becomes God. The sufferer experiences the pain as religion. They do not seek our religion as an explanation for the recurring hurt, but rather that hurt is the religion.
I very often got the impression that I was a sort of game for the pain. Whenever I felt like I couldn't go on anymore, it took a short break. When I didn't want to go on anymore and there was nothing to be done, the pain would leave for a day. As though it just wanted to use me as its plaything. Like how a cat plays with a mouse it has just caught. Of course, the mouse doesn't stand a chance against the cat. But it can actually influence how interesting it is to the cat. The more intensely it struggles, the more fun it becomes for the cat
I've decided not to let the pain defeat me. But I must comply with it. It is always there, and it picks up on everything. The parallels between it and the omniscient

Christian God are surprising, and sometimes terrifying. Prayer would be the wrong term to use, but when I hold an internal dialogue, it's with the pain, not with God.

To this day I don't know what it all looks like from the pain's perspective. Even though I have often thought about it, I can't put together a real sketch of its motives. It doesn't need me for anything. I don't feel that I am ultimately the host for its existence. So I have never found a better model than that of pure despotism.

Still, this thought experiment makes very clear how the behaviour that I consider to be the best way to address the disease actually looks. If I am subjected to pressure, I must promptly build up the appropriate counterpressure. If the pressure is so strong that I can't prepare any sufficient response, then it's important to make myself as unassailable as possible. To speak figuratively, it would be best to become liquid, because the strongest fist cannot hold fast to a liquid - it will simply trickle out between the fingers.

One could imagine the pain as a large fist raining down on me from the sky. I throw myself helplessly onto the ground, try to be as shapeless as possible, and simply wait out the worst of storms. Once the wind subsides - because its power has been exhausted for the moment - I lift myself up to defy the weakening tempest. It's quite practical to imagine things this way. At the moment when the pain is worst, the body instinctively curls into the foetal position. Rolled up to offer as little room for attack as possible. In these moments I always draw back on two different mantras. First I think to myself over and over, "Go away!" Once I feel like the pain is on the retreat, I append it with a little, "I am stronger!" It took a very long time to get used to this autosuggestion, but it works.

If we imagine pain as a tremendous arm pushing down on us, it luckily seems that it has to adhere to the laws of physics. The stronger the muscle pushing down on you, the faster it overacidifies and it can no longer be supplied with oxygen. Indeed, it is too strong for you to defend yourself against it. But it will run out of air and need a break, too. It is during that break that you can decide for yourself whether you will stay lying down or if you will stand up again.

The Question of Condition

The harmless question, "How are you?", has become a gauntlet that repeats itself every day. Almost no one who asks about another's well-being actually wants to know anything about it. And nobody wants to answer, either. Still, polite truisms are a frequent ritual for starting conversations. Where I'm from, indignation tends to manifest in the following manner:
Q: "Wie isset?" (How's it going?)
A: "Muss!" (It's gotta!)
Chatterboxes will occasionally opt for the longer expression, "It's gotta! And you?». Humorous contemporaries like to counter with, "It was going yesterday." But actually, the only permissible responses are, "I'm okay", "I'm good", and maybe "I'm fine". In my case, a rather more philosophical reply would be more appropriate, such as, "That's a complex question to which I cannot currently give a simple answer." But responses like that are usually best left for the doctor's office. Even good friends often ask me without actually having time for a real answer.
There was a long period of time when I would have had to answer any questions about how I was doing with a truthful, and distinct, "Shitty!" People don't do that, of course. But why not? For one, some may be reluctant to use such vocabulary. One doesn't really want to actually tell everyone - and possibly quite verbosely - what's wrong and how they're actually doing. And lastly, most of the time the person asking doesn't really want an answer. It's a ritual that has gotten out of control. Androids working on a spaceship can answer the question with a

simple, "I am functioning within normal parameters." Normal people are caught in a maelstrom of absentmindedness. An undertow that begins with a supposed act of politeness. Yet the opposite of "good" is "well-intentioned". How polite is it ultimately to begin a conversation with a question to which the asker doesn't expect an answer? The polite phrase in turn becomes the actual act of impoliteness.

Yet no matter how correct or incorrect my philosophical perception is, it won't at all change that this question of feigned interest in one's own well-being in life will continue to be asked. And because it happens a lot more frequently than once per year, it's worth the effort of thinking about it. Many times this question has only confused me. I couldn't exactly formulate how I was really doing. At the time when I was asked I may not have had any acute pain at all. An hour before, sure. Or the pain disappeared thanks to an Imigran injection. On top of that, I may have woken up a number of times in the night because of the pain.

No, in moments like those I don't know how I'm doing. I'm happy when I realise that I am, that I actually exist. How should I answer the question now? After all, the answer doesn't matter, because the question is nothing more than an empty phrase.

What did matter to me was the fact that I also confused myself when this question was posed to me. Now what should I do? First it's helpful to tell whether the asker has any sincere or professional interest, or none at all. Is the question being asked by a doctor, therapist, or concerned friends? Or from a neighbour who happened to see me while out shopping?

In the second instance - the cliché - I tend to reply with the most negative of the generally acceptable answers: "I'm fine." I could also opt to volley with, "I'm fine. And you?" However, in the event that the asker does not tick in the same way I do, I could cause a possible double spiral with an uncontrollable undertow effect. So it's better to just leave it.

I tried for a time to deflect the question with humour, like replying, "Is it bad people who are always doing well, or the other way around?" I always preferred that over a positive answer that didn't match up with the truth.

Whosoever can do it naturally has an easy time of it. The ghost is gone with a simple, "Good." "Pretty good" also works for those who want to weaken it a bit. An empty phrase should be treated like one. It is not the specific asker's fault that it causes such puzzlement in me. As is often the case, one's own evaluation is also the pertinent and impressionable factor.

Now I'd like to go back to the first instance. We're asked by somebody with actual interest, be it a doctor, a therapist, or a friend. Those who work in a healing profession have naturally earned an honest answer, because anything else would not help the matter. I have since begun asking friends if they want a polite or an honest answer. And that works extraordinarily well.

But no matter how much I prepare myself, what steps I take or concoct, I simply don't like being asked about how I'm doing.

Two-Class Society

How often is frequent, how intense is severe, and how much is too much?

Pain cannot be measured. It very likely, almost to the point of certainty, differs from one person to the next. Years in the self-help group have shown me that every sufferer has their own cluster headache that can also morph over time. Along with the many minor differences that also cannot be measured on a scale, there is also one major difference.

Have you ever fainted?

All pain patients - pain because of headache, back pain, rheumatic pain, or cancer pain - are asked to measure the severity of their pain on a scale from 0 to 10, whereby 0 always means no pain, and 10 equals the greatest pain imaginable. Now, there should be a certain unanimity about what no pain feels like. But from my own observations I know that the opposite end of the scale behaves quite differently. How is one supposed to know what the greatest pain imaginable is without having experienced it?

My personal scale is ordered as follows:

0. No pain
1. More like discomfort than pain
2. Slight, but distinct pain
3. Pain
4. Pain that does not allow me to concentrate on anything else
5. Pain that still allows me to be social if absolutely necessary
6. Things get really unpleasant from here on out
7. The pain begins to eliminate all other perception. I no longer notice whether it's hot or cold, even if it's way too cold
8. Loss of fine motor skills, I can no longer tie my shoes
9. I am not receptive, I do not register the sensation of touch
10. Frenzy, self-harm, fainting

I did not invent these steps in the scale. I have personally experienced them. Each and every one of them, and many more. Experiencing the last step - fainting from pain - splits cluster headache sufferers into two distinct camps. Whether or not the sufferer has woken up on the cold kitchen tiles in the middle of the night or not changes their perspective. This very experience shaped my attitude greatly.

I used to believe that it "has to leave somehow". Slave away until the cows come home. Grit your teeth. I don't have anything anyway. It only hurts. And then it came one time - my acquaintance with the cold kitchen floor. I had no idea how I had gotten to that point, nor how long I had been lying there. It was still dark outside, and it was cold. My eyes opened again and I found myself over-chilled on the floor. I was happy that my head didn't hurt anymore, that I was alone, and that nobody had seen me like that. And I was afraid because I was alone and nobody was there to help me.

"Personal responsibility" is the key phrase. We should be responsible in the way we treat ourselves. Still, we often don't: "Don't make such a fuss! Things will turn out okay!" In the meantime I do make a fuss and pay attention to my strain threshold, because my body has made it clear to me in no uncertain terms that sometimes things don't turn out okay.

That frightening first moment of helplessness permanently helps one find the brakes, and then to step on them when need be.

"The world goes on," as the saying goes. Yet those who have passed out from pain learned that sometimes the world doesn't go on. It's just the end, curtains, end of story.

The German band Wolfsheim expressed the following in their 2003 single "Kein Zurück" ("No Going Back"):

The world is beautiful and full of colours.
Until one day you realise,
That not every goodbye,
Means there will be another hello.

Even though songwriter Peter Heppner's words are certainly about something else entirely, I find them profoundly fitting.

Quo Vadis?

You are what you are and you have what you have. But what good does that do in a normal life? Taking stock, the following is revealed:
I am sick and will remain so. My supply of medication is secured and my doctors even respond to e-mails in an emergency. I am known personally at my pharmacy and medical store. Nobody puts obstacles in my way. The logistics are there. My friends and family also know the score. Stories are shared at the self-help group, and my yoga class also promotes balance. Both also provide social contacts for free.
It almost sounds like a beautiful life. And it would be in an advertisement. The pharmaceutical companies like to use ads to suggest that after you take their medications, you'll feel even better than if you had never been sick at all.
But stepping back from the rosy world of marketing into the not-so-colourful reality, the first sentence always applies: I am sick and will remain so. And a regulated supply does not equal the elimination of symptoms.

There is no doubt that work and relationships are two central elements to any person's life. How does the disease, and working with it, specifically fit into one's professional life? (Observations as to how disease and relationships intermingle will follow in the next chapter.)
To be up front about it, work and cluster headache do not go together in many ways. It is quite exhausting to reconcile the two in some way. And it's hard for me to not get angry about this topic. It's even harder to find out what, or whom, I should even be angry at.

But I'd like to start from the beginning. My academic career was unremarkable and linear. After kindergarten and primary school I attended the Gymnasium, and graduated with a diploma after the normal period. I performed my community service thereafter. Then, with my university entrance qualifications in my pocket I attended the Ruhr University Bochum to study mechanical engineering. The extremely impersonal studies at this grey, concrete palace was not an environment entirely conducive to my own sense of happiness. I also had to involuntarily leave my parents' home around this time, and I was left to digest a not-so-pretty separation.

I counteracted this first bump in my life by changing colleges and attending the Bochum University of Applied Sciences. In retrospect I was not particularly worried about the future for the following period of time, to put it mildly. I worked odd jobs more than I studied. It got to the point that I was only attending classes once per semester, and that was just to enroll again. I was what is referred to as an eternal student. But because I was getting good work at the time, I wasn't much bothered by it.

I led my life away from a regulated nine-to-five office job. I wasn't really a dropout who sails around the world, but more like a soldier of fortune, though not an unhappy one. German TV-Truckers Franz Meersdonk and Günther Willers had had in impact on me. I got my truck driver's license and became the Jobbing King at a forwarding company. I was doing well, my job was fun, and I got the necessary respect in the form of cars fresh out of the factory. It was a nice time. It could have just gone on like that, and I would have stuck with the job. But when the company moved in the late 1990s, things would go differently from then on. I had to commute a very inconvenient distance.

At this time the EDP industry was booming and was now known as IT. Companies were all employing someone who knew how PCs tick. In the current of this IT boom I was easily able to switch from trucker to IT support. I actually knew enough about computers to be able to hold my own at my first job in the field. I also learned quickly on the job and was even able to improve my professional skills.

Admittedly, I was still an officially registered student. Yet I had not seen in the inside of a lecture hall in a long time, and I had taken just as few exams in all that time. I was now nearly 30 years old and was used to my life as a soldier of fortune. Nothing unusual happened to me. To look at it practically, I had at the very least arranged for my own survival, but not my future. I knew that, too, but I masterfully suppressed it. After all, I didn't have the worst job at a large computer retailer in Dortmund.

While this job went very smoothly, and I had a partner in my personal life whom I really wanted to be with, the disease slowly reached its hand out to me. I woke up ever more frequently in the night with infernal headaches. I tried one common headache medication after another, and in greater quantities, to no avail. Despite an entire series of tests, not one doctor was able to say what was wrong with me.

At least I knew that it wasn't a brain tumour, which I originally had a distinct and great fear of. Because these extremely severe pains always struck at the same location, I was certain that it must be something in my head that doesn't belong there. To this very day I still have the MR scans of my brain that thankfully don't show any such foreign bodies.

Three things then happened shortly thereafter. The pain not only came at night, but also during the day. The gold rush of the IT boom was over, and my company slowly began laying off all workers who didn't have children. This left me out on the street. Plagued by pain and unemployed, I no longer offered my partner any serious prospects and in this part of my life, too, I was soon out on a limb. (I will explain why I accepted this decision so easily in a later chapter.)

With that, my life collapsed into a shambles astonishingly quickly. Just turned 30, no professional prospects, and suffering from an unknown disease, I sat at home alone every night, knowing less and less what to do with my life.

I thus found myself in the middle of a classic spiral of depression. My finances were approaching zero. My bank account was empty, my car was broken, and I had absolutely no idea how I would go on. It took a drastic turn of events in the form of a diagnosis of my disease just for me to get any kind of outlook on the future. After I finally knew what the enemy in my head was years later, I could deal with it first and then come up with ideas for a professional existence.

My CV was, of course, a disaster. With no completed higher education and with holes bigger than Swiss cheese, I had no need to form any realistic expectations of regular employment. Working independently was the fallback. So I tried holding my own by programming websites and repairing computers. It's no surprise that starting out is always difficult. In my case, however, continuing was just as hard. Anyone plagued by severe, constant pain for an average of three out of twelve months in the year cannot generate the finances to survive. I often had to cancel appointments, or hurried to the customer's toilet to take a shot of Imigran.

That was better than banging my throbbing head against the wall. In addition, the question wasn't how well that works, but for how long. Addled from the Imigran, I made more than one mistake and at least one time it would almost not have been able to be hidden or amended. I took this as a red flag, because the very real recourse claims following one serious mistake could not be my objective.

However, this episode was a step in the right direction. Thanks to contacts I had made and my disability which was now recognised, it was possible for me to have an education individually funded by the labour committee. Two years after signing the agreement, I passed my final exams and have since been a digital and print media designer: design and technology.

I had tinkered with computers for years, and in that time I learned that educated technicians are not necessarily more competent than I am. So I spoke before the Chamber of

Industry and Commerce and was given the chance to take an external exam. Four months later I passed this test as well. Now I can not only call myself a media designer, but also a system integration technician.

It sounds good, and it also felt very good. Now everything could be good, or at the very least better. But, sadly, it wasn't. After my last exams I felt like I had fallen into a hole. Yet the headache journal quite prosaically revealed that the number of headache attacks had continued to rise one month before. If the exams had been just one or two weeks later, the result probably would have looked different. And although time and feeling would have been kicking off again, my head was very stubbornly thwarting my plans, because what followed was one of the most intense episodes up until that time.

Following my small round of exams was an episode at the epicentre of which I could not sleep for one entire night over 18 straight weeks, and experienced up to six attacks per day. At the end I had a new medication schedule and multiple treatments that helped me get back on my feet. I ultimately landed in competent facilities and was able to learn a lot about coping strategies and acceptance of the disease.

Regardless, it would take well over a year for me to turn my inward perspective back outward. That is where I stand now. Despite my handicap brought on by chronic illness, I now have two professions and am no longer without any higher education.

But my life story is by no means a textbook example. It will surely continue to be a source of furrowed brows and shaking heads among the decision-makers at HR departments. This doesn't bode well for my competitive chances. Not to mention that I misjudged myself with my choice of career. The employers of media designers and IT specialists are quite frequently small agencies who are, in practice, at the mercy of the needs, desires, and moods of the customer. In the advertisement the customer provides the required materials at the last minute at the earliest, but still sets the deadline for "yesterday". Of course this results in irregular work hours and peak periods of stress that I am no longer built for.

The modern world is a society of output that I can't keep up with anymore. Because I was a soldier of fortune in my first decade on the workforce, I unfortunately never put down roots that allow me to remain employed despite my disability. So I try finding a new field to work in. However, what that field exactly is has remained unclear both to myself and to anyone else. My disability cannot be fathomed, not by me and especially not by a third party. After all, pain cannot be seen and I have no way of predicting when the next episode that is so intense that I am completely unemployable once more will occur.

I only know that even in symptom-free times, I can no longer compete with healthy candidates. Even though cluster headache isn't a psychosomatic disease, every form of stress and overstimulation has palpable negative consequences. I have to consider whether that suits me or not in the interest of self-responsibility. I should even try not getting angry at the fact that I can no longer do things the way I would like to. That, too, is a form of stress and it leads to spirals with a current pulling in the wrong direction.

Presently, I'm fascinated by people who don't have a career in order to accumulate as much material profit as possible, but rather who pursue a career that fulfils them. Naturally I would be happy to not depend on material things, but career and wealth don't constitute worthy objectives for me anymore. I can't imagine being any happier with 5,000 euros per month than I would be with 1,500 euros. But someone with 1,500 euros is happier than they would be with 500. With income that low, the person is too close to the poverty line, and by definition they are even below it. Great restrictions have to be set, and a broken washing machine becomes an immense problem, and the result is more stress.

Isn't it wonderful that a severe, chronic disease that causes permanent disability makes one into a more frugal person?

Now to get back to the harsh world of work. Nearly every job ad seeks applicants who are as flexible and durable as possible. I have even found the word "stress-resistant" as a requirement before. The society of output cannot be proclaimed any clearer than that. When I read such ads all I can do is let out a quiet sigh. I cannot meet these requirements without hurting myself in the process. But then I keep on reading until I find the attributes I seek: "diligent" or "thorough".

So why not just go back to school for a new trade? Because I'm not a bricklayer with bad knees, or a construction worker with a bad back. I'm severely disabled. I have actually been invited to such interviews after my benefits expired upon 78 weeks of unemployment. And the problem wasn't that nobody wanted to help out. Rather, it's finding something suitable. To exaggerate slightly, I suffer from a social intolerance.

This situation always results in creative to ludicrous ideas: professions often beyond the realm of most normal people, like glass eye designer, stonecutter, or shepherd suddenly seem quite interesting. But there are far too few open positions in these fields, and so the ideas remain ideas.

For a long time there was no clear solution to this dilemma in sight. The only thing that was certain was that trying nothing is also a conscious decision - and the worst. You can never be one hundred per cent sure that something is going to work. But you can be absolutely certain that doing nothing will never work. Either way, a solution can suddenly appear out of thin air. Things can happen that can neither be planned nor predicted.

This is the fortune that befell me when I ultimately found a suitable job. When all is said and done, my only confession is that I am not built for a full-time, 40-hour workweek, and perhaps I never will be. But this applies to all jobs, and I can't hold that against them. Once it was out of style, I was able to learn that there are still professions in which a human being is treated like one instead of walking capital.

Relationship Issues

When I talk about this topic it's easy to get angry, but it's much harder to be clear as to what I'm actually angry about.

I live alone. I have lived alone for most of my life. I have no dog, and there isn't a ficus to be found in my flat. If I had a dog, I guarantee it would have had to do its business right here in the flat from time to time. Every potted plant would have wilted. Cacti wouldn't stand a chance.

When I was living with my parents I unfortunately never learned what a happy family looks like. So as a young man I had no ambitions to make one for myself. After some adventures, some significant and some not, I found myself in a situation in which there was a woman whom I felt I wanted to grow old with. Wild oats had been sown, the sea had calmed down, and I felt like I was in the right port. It was sort of the wrong time to get sick, but that's the way it happened. Night after night these pains, and nobody who could explain them to me. I thought it was a brain tumour and was no longer very good at creatively planning a future. My partner had (and probably still has) a distinct sense of security. A civil servant who always had about two months' wages saved up in her checking account. That doesn't fit particularly well into the life plan of someone who's just starting to give up.

I lost my job promptly thereafter, and I felt thoroughly abandoned by everything that can abandon someone. Job gone, woman gone, and always the pain that not one doctor could explain. From my perspective at the time, I was the textbook example of a social failure. It would take years for me to dig myself out of this hole. Why bother talking to another female? So I can get a headache during a date?

I since learned that it was cluster headache, and I had medication so that I could at the very least deal with it better. And there actually was another female who crossed my path and who enticed my spirits to come back out of the mausoleum that they had retreated into. But these spirits had to endure a long struggle with my mind. Over - no joke - the span of one whole year my journal is filled with frequent, imploring entries. "Forget it!" I ordered myself with changing reasoning. But it ended the way it had to end. Ultimately, the beguiling aroma won.

She, a highly energetic and egomaniacal dragon. I, the opposite, and sometimes too careful. Whereas she considered the impossible possible, I would let an opportunity pass me by out of excessive precaution. This combination can make a strong team, and for a while it worked for us. With her I was able to get a few things moving that I would have needed much longer to initiate if I had been alone.

In my last serious relationship I had learned that the partner's problems are always amplified when they sympathise. The other's pains also hurt them. But when it comes to cluster headache, the pain of an attack just has to be accepted. In that moment I don't want consolation, I don't want soothing words or any type of closeness. I am alone with the raging in my head, and that's how I want it. And so every time, I snub whomever is there at my side at the time. It may happen multiple times per day.

Yet when the attack is over and the pain has faded away, and I - wrung out like I just ran a marathon - push my bottle of oxygen away from me, it looks very different. Even though it was long ago, I can still remember well how nice it is to not be alone in those moments, and how much power an embrace can give when it happens.

Interestingly enough, I've always been more attracted to woman of commanding size whom I can look in the eye without having to bend my neck. It also adds a more protective nature to embraces, and that can't function effectively when my partner is a head shorter than me. I have to be able to hold myself tight instead.

This also requires a partner who sits next to me unaffected, and then acts like a commando and is there exactly when I need them. New lovers do this very well, but as routine drags on it becomes more difficult. At least my fortune was not meant to last that long. Our differing natures, which at first had made us strong, were still unable to endure a longer pain episode in the end.

I felt challenged and did not want to surrender myself to the constant pain. I ended up taking too much Imigran as a result, and ultimately found myself in an even deeper hole. I simply overdid it. After all, the opposite of good is well-intentioned. The rest of the story all boils down to a classical allocation of roles. A strong woman looks for an even stronger man. And I was not able to hold that role in the long term.

For the sake of emphasis, a partner who has her own tendencies to be the alpha provides the necessary lack of empathy in order to be able to just watch an episode happen. At some point, the driveling rag that remains will no longer be enough for her.

The partner who does not need a dominant man by her side is very likely to empathetic to be able to endure all of the constant suffering next to her. And so I implore to all sufferers blessed with a partner in the spectrum between the two poles above, and who constantly strengthens them and doesn't get in their way: treat these people with a little more care than somebody should treat the person they love.

And what about those who throw in the towel and vanish into thin air? Well, I'm certain that this isn't a problem specific to clusterheads. One could be paraplegic or go blind from an accident, or suffer from life-changing chronic diseases like multiple sclerosis, Parkinson's, epilepsy, or dementia. With the cards dealt to me, I am not the person I once was. And if the sufferer could choose, they would get rid of their disease. The partner has that choice. Can I be disappointed in my partner simply for doing what I would do if I had the option?

I didn't see it that way at the time, of course. I felt as though somebody had torn my heart out and pushed me off of the narrow plank on which I had been treading through life up until then. Pushed me into a freefall toward eternal oblivion. But nobody is stopping me from reassessing a situation. I do not feel good about it, but I feel better.

Perspectives

"If you were to be silent, you could be helped," is a phrase the deeper meaning of which has long eluded me. Acceptance of a life-changing disease takes time, but it's necessary.

Men do not stumble over mountains, but over molehills.
Confucius

More than Pain

It is documented in a medical assessment written about me that I use uncommon terms and descriptions for my symptoms. One astonishingly long assessment in particular must at least have taken longer to write than the time spent with me on site in person. In any case, my uncommon choice of phrasing, according to the assessment, is that I have described my situation as a "complete artwork", and specifically that I must have coined the term "sleep paranoia". It's not enough for an entire work of art, but I did exhibit some symptoms, it continues.

The assessment states that sleep disorders, concentration disorders, verbal disorders, forgetfulness, and a long-term loss of libido are direct and indirect consequences of the frequent pain. If the pain just lasts long enough, a decrease in physical and mental performance can hardly be prevented. This is all coupled with anxiety and panic attacks. The resulting depression is almost unavoidable.

The following independent symptoms are listed specifically:

- Sleep disorder G47.0
- Concentration, reduced F98.8
- Light cognitive impairment F06.7
- Other speaking and linguistic disorders R47.8
- Phobic disorders F40.-
- Depressive episode F32.-

So there's a lot to treat!

But still not enough. Then there's the alternation between aggression and apathy, auto-aggression with a tendency toward self-harm, lack of motivation and other vegetative disorders, as well as photosensitivity and the aforementioned solar intolerance.

This part of the complete artwork is solely based on the foundation of the constant pain. My constant struggle for a tolerable body mass index is not directly based on it. The pain can't do anything for my tendency for obesity, but it weakens the necessary discipline. There are some medications that don't have a positive impact on this either. Quite logically, this leads to a pain episode also manifesting in weight gain. Actually it's entirely unclear whether my rheumatic pain that has primarily arisen during the cold season for some years now is in any way associated with the cluster headache. Still, they don't help my overall well-being in any case.

That alone would be enough, but the complete artwork includes another component. I grew up under a father who was diagnosed with a narcissistic personality disorder that, year after year, met more criteria for somebody with compulsive hoarding. He is also an alcoholic. I am not saying that he would suffer from these diseases, because others do that already.

Most people will be familiar with the notorious image of a garbage hoarder. For us, it started out with a basement piled up to the ceiling, and then the first garage, followed by the second, ultimately ending with the entire house. Shortly before I turned my back on my parents' house my father began storing our regular household trash in the garage so that he could look through it all again.

Not everyone may know what somebody with narcissistic personality disorder looks like, however. Such people have an overblown sense of importance, and they hope to take on and earn a special position. They exhibit exploitative behaviour and a lack of empathy.

People affected by it also show marked sensitivity to criticism, which they often understand globally. This evokes in them a sense of rage, embarrassment, or discouragement. That's why it's not uncommon for a web of intrigue to be woven among the family in particular in order to cast themselves in the "right light". Their perception of actual circumstances is often severely blurred, and is either beautified for the benefit of the narcissistic personality, parts of reality are deliberately falsified, or omitted altogether. The goal is to restore the respect that the narcissist believes has been toppled. This is often done through great self-pity, and combatted with complaining and begging to arouse other peoples' worry and reinforce the narcissist's own innocence. When I learned about the diagnosis and read its symptoms for the first time, it was clear that every trait is present.

So how must one envision such a person? Like someone without pride, and who pays no consideration to anyone and anything! For example, my progenitor got a dog and took it on a visit to his mother - my grandmother. She asked him not to bring the dog into the house. At the time my grandmother was an old lady well over 70 years old, and she simply wasn't comfortable with it. It certainly wouldn't any inconvenience for the dog, since he was allowed to stay out in the yard. My father simply didn't care about his mother's own wishes, and he brought the dog into her home. That in itself isn't the end of the world, but it's a typical example of how people like that behave. Coupled with a propensity for bravado and the tendency to put things in the "right" light, this results in a lack of understanding of circumstances in one's own environment even after decades.

To give another example: in my childhood bedroom my father installed an adjustable panel under the ceiling that could be lowered, and a race car track and model train set were mounted onto it. It was cool, no doubt. Admittedly, it was also something special that nobody else had. So I still have uncles, aunts, and other relatives who believe that my progenitor actually took care of his children.

In this instance I actually got to benefit, but my father did not construct this extraordinary kid's room to make friends out of my sister and me. Rather, it served as a vehicle for his self-presentation. The entire thing was displayed happily. The methodology was actually effective, too, because there are people who still remember it and the thing they actually draw from it is, "You kids actually had it really good."

Yet those same people either forgot, or did not notice at the time, that the same actor would have a drop too much at every family event and then take the wheel with two kids in the back seat. You could also ask them who ended up giving water to the dog. It wasn't him, of course. It was my grandmother.

This lack of empathy was also present in our father-son relationship, and it was very distinct as early as my childhood. No matter what I did and how much I tried, it was not good enough for my father or he simply wasn't interested, regardless what it was about. I even "failed" when sweeping the garage and he would just do it over again. There was simply nothing that met up to his standards. The fact that he treated other people the same way did not make things any more bearable for me as a kid.

Luckily, the worst aggressors are still just people, and they are neither perfect nor infallible. My progenitor was a competent craftsman, but once things got moving he couldn't find where to start. So in my youth I turned to things that he had no reference to and that he couldn't judge. When I was twelve years old I bought my first computer, a Commodore C64. It let me create a world free from my father's criticism.

Yet the ramifications remain frighteningly deeply rooted to this day. When someone acts like my father around me, I have to take a deep breath to prevent any spontaneous acts of defiance from myself.

These experiences didn't exactly work wonders for my self-confidence. Now, with my sickness, I'm no longer able to meet expectations. At least not for the time being. This is where childhood conditioning meets neurological disorder, amplifying all of their psychosomatic effects.

We have a complete artwork, a damn tall and wobbly Jenga tower that is hard to stabilise. But hard is not the same as impossible. Discovering this connection was shocking, but also a source of motivation. My father is the last person I want to see affecting my life. Even today he still terrorises parts of my family, and has disrupted their cohesion for the long term. The last thing I can allow is for him to worm his way back into my life from afar, even though as a child I never learned how to build up the self-confidence that is now required to endure this disease. Now I have to. Thankfully, adversity and anger are powerful motivators!

My personal foundation of the complete artwork is supplemented by some general effects of chronic illnesses and disabilities. The State Self-Help Association of NRW e.V. and the Network Office for Women and Girls with Disability/Chronic Illness NRW are currently conducting a study on depression and psychosomatic disorders caused by disability/chronic illness, funded by the AOK Rheinland/Hamburg and AOK NordWest health insurance companies. So far the study has shown that, regardless of the type of illness, an entire range of effects manifest in all sorts of patients. When the first results of this long-term study were presented during a presentation at the 8th roundtable discussion of the Association of Statutory Health Insurance Physicians Westfalen-Lippe, I was sitting in the auditorium and felt as though it was my story being presented up there.

One physical symptom which I am obviously not the only person subjected to is known as general fatigue. This in itself entails a long list of physical problems:

- Loneliness and isolation: If the number of attacks is so high that I will most likely have to expect an attack in public, I keep my public presence to a minimum.
- Overload: If I lose too much time because of frequent pain, this sensation sets in very quickly.
- Helplessness and fear: I never know when it will begin and when it will stop again. I can no longer act as though I'm reacting to symptoms.

- Fear that the disease will return: Even in symptom-free times, the sword of Damocles that is the next attack is constantly hanging over me. I have experienced the sudden recurrence of the disease all too often.
- Fear of becoming a burden to my partner, and a lack of understanding by my partner: Because I learned how to be unimportant when I was still a child, this applies to me far more than I would like.
- Lack of sensitivity from doctors: I'm fortunate to have left this behind me.
- Working with officials or bureaucratic structures: This was often quite difficult because of office employees' ignorance of disability- and disease-specific strains and needs. Since I began owning my own disabled person identification, however, these strength-sapping encounters are much more uncommon now. The other person's level of knowledge doesn't increase, but with an ID it's clearly assumed that the impairments are serious.
- Work and finances: Money generally improves one's scope of opportunities. A lack of money traps one in the opposite situation. Living with chronic diseases is thus distinguished by lifelong limitations, deprivations, and exhausting encounters.

The World Health Organisation (WHO) defines the conditions for health as follows: "The prerequisites for health are peace, shelter, education, social security, social relations, food, income, the empowerment of women, a stable eco-system, sustainable resource use, social justice, respect for human rights, and equity." But under such conditions it's hard to develop and maintain the vital energy and joie de vivre, energy, and optimism that make it easier to deal with sickness-induced stress. I have come to understand it as a challenge to work out and apply my own management strategies despite this.

15 Minutes

One of my most concrete handicaps as a clusterhead is the lack of ability to plan my life.
Time passes me by when I'm not doing well. Time even passes me by when I'm doing well, because I have to keep my disease organised.
Because the disease is not sufficiently well-known and doesn't have a terrifying nature like Parkinson's or multiple sclerosis, the fight for acceptance takes up far too much time. I have long thought that it is time completely wasted for no reason. But because the disease and the pain associated with it cannot just be wished away, I have the option to expose myself to everything that may come my way, like a cork in the ocean. Or I can prepare myself, as I describe in the chapter "Logistics of a Chronic Illness". In the meantime I have learned that the effort has been, and continues to be, worth it. I simply have to keep depositing into this account for a while before any profits are generated.
Yet it still eats a lot of time. And sometimes it eats too much.
The average nighttime attack lasts about 30 minutes. What exactly do these 30 minutes mean? I measure it as the net pain period: the specific period in which I sit with my breathing mask over my nose, next to my bottle of oxygen, trying to breathe peacefully and evenly, and to remain calm despite the pain. After a few hundred times I actually became rather trained to it, and I'm getting ever better at it. I was asleep before these 30 minutes, then I had to wake up, and afterward the pain has forced me awake to the point that I can't just fall back asleep right away. This equates to an interruption of my sleep of at least 60 minutes.
When something like that happens occasionally, the body can learn to cope with it. But when it happens every night, it can deplete the body. I ultimately torture myself. My own experience tells me that if I want to compensate for

the disruption to my night's rest, it's not enough to just make up for the lost time. This time can certainly be doubled, leaving us with two hours. Together with the disruption, 30-minute pain attacks mean that one would have to wake up an entire three hours later than someone who treats their body responsibly.

That's the calculation for one nighttime attack. What does the projection for up to three attacks look like? This adds up over a number of weeks. My personal record sits at 18 weeks during which I could not sleep one entire night. If anyone is able to maintain a normal schedule despite that, I respectfully tip my hat to them. I cannot do it. My journal includes this entry for a day following three nighttime attacks: "I can still feel the imprints from the freight train that must have run me over in the night."

In addition to the nights are the days. Here I have the advantage of being able to recognise an attack in advance through its warning signs. At night the pain usually tears me out of my sleep. During the day I feel the harbingers, because my attacks have an advance period of about 15 minutes. These 15 minutes are also the only thing I can take stock of. I don't know if I'll be better in a half-hour, and I am rarely able to make a prediction. Cluster attacks come from out of the blue with this little warning sign, at any possible and impossible opportunity. While taking a walk, riding my bicycle, going to the movies, taking a holiday or going to a funeral. And yes, the first night spent with a wonderful woman.

Upon experiencing it hundreds of times, I've grown cautious. Sometimes I'm directly on the border of paranoia. At least I only very begrudgingly make appointments in the midst of an attack, and am quite reluctant to set a schedule. All too often have I not been able to observe appointments, or had to cancel or at least interrupt them, because of entirely unpredictable headache attacks. Too frequently have I crawled up in some corner or hidden in bathrooms. For some years now these moments have lost

some of their terror thanks to my medication, and Imigran in particular.
But the 15 minutes are still there. I will never know how I'll be doing in half an hour.

Headache

When people are worried about something, they like to say, "This is giving me a headache." And so an everyday colloquialism ends up breaking the neck of the seriously, chronically ill. Tumours aren't thrown around quite so lightly. "Tumour is when you laugh regardless," would be considered dark as night.
There are a number of expressions found in everyday speech that all reveal how external influences affect well-being. For example, an uncomfortable conversation can "make your stomach queasy", and a fright can "make your heart go up to your mouth", or even "curdle your blood". If something makes us mad, this can cause make our "veins pop" and we could "jump out of our skin". Then it that doesn't help, we're "sick of it". We also get "pale from fear", "red with rage", and our hair can "stand on end".
These psychosomatic connections have merged into colloquial speech. And yet the headache has been taken a step further. Headaches have become established as an international excuse for the displeasure at physical proximity. This leads to such cheap jokes as, "Here darling, your Aspirin. - But I don't have a headache. - Great, then we can shag." And the schlager song "I've Got a Headache this Evening" by Ireen Sheer stayed on the charts for weeks, and to this day it remains a standard every time you want to go nine-pin bowling.
Headache is an accepted, momentary ailment, but nothing more. It can even serve as an excuse and apology. It is tolerated as the result of excessive alcohol consumption, but is not considered a serious sickness.

It goes without saying that these are indeed headaches in both cases. Yet this terminology, and its sometimes ridiculous social entanglements, are at fault for the trivialisation - and thus the lack of acceptance - of the headache as a serious illness. Personally, I would much prefer it if the WHO were to use the term erythroprosopalgia in its diagnosis classifications instead of "cluster headache".

When somebody is asked what disease they have, the patient experiences clear differences in the intensity of their concern. Cancer always gives way to great concern, as do Parkinson's or multiple-sclerosis. This is where you spontaneously think, "Thank God I don't have that." And that does not happen with the term "headache". The initial thought here is more along the lines of, "Yeah, I've had that." This small change in perception and reaction by the other party has ultimately had a major impact on people suffering from it.

There is no escape from this vicious cycle, let alone the stupid sickness. All the same, public relations work and the associated clarification have improved the situation somewhat.

Turmoil

There is one characteristic that likely sets cluster headache apart from all other classes of headache: the unease!

No, I don't want to lie down. And I don't want to have my peace. What I do want in that moment, though, is to be left alone. I don't want anyone to see me like that. In the moment when I'm experiencing pain, I feel naked and vulnerable. That is when I want to be left to myself, and in that situation I express myself on a spectrum ranging from blatantly obvious to harsh. It's hard to be nice when I feel like there's a red hot knife stuck in my eye.

Over the years I have learned to control my motoric unease, as it tends to intensify the pain. Now I simply try to strain only the muscles that are absolutely necessary, and not to spasm under any circumstances. The strategies imparted by yoga help me here.

But the tendency to respond to pain with pain in turn is deeply rooted. Every attack arouses memories of times when I didn't have any medication to alleviate the ache, and when I was entirely exposed to the raging in my skull for hours on end. Sometimes I still feel the painful knuckles that used to bleed when I would punch the wall during an attack. These circumstances do not make one into a gentle lamb, and instead develop an inclination to devolve into a hooligan.

This energy can be used to get excited about everything and everyone. There are certainly enough reasons for it. Doctors who can't help someone, friends who don't understand them, and jobs that have been lost. One does not get a lot of that. But it has also taken a long time for me to adopt this view. Nowadays I try to collect the energy and consolidate it so that I can stand back up when the time is right.

Should I have an attack during an occasion I cannot immediately flee from, that notorious question is posed to me: "Are you not feeling well? Don't you want to lie down?" So I always have to hold myself back a lot simply to say, "No," and not overreact by shouting in response.

The oft expressed assumption that headaches have psychosomatic causes goes in a similar direction.

I quote: "Are you feeling burdened by something that could be irritating your head?"

The fact that I suffer from constant headaches is almost the only thing that is burdening me. Even though it's well-intentioned, kind, and serious, IT'S ANNOYING! Nobody would even think to ask me questions like that and then make corresponding suggestions if I suffered from a more proper disease like cancer, multiple sclerosis, or Parkinson's.

The constant headaches can easily be the cause for a wide variety of other symptoms. The headaches themselves, however, have no mental causes. I have been absolutely certain of this for years. Too often do I experience attacks at times when they have no reason to occur.

Self-Harm

A number of symptoms result in self-destructive behaviour. It is usually interpreted as a method for alleviating stress, rage, and self-hatred. But we clusterheads are also a little different from everyone else. Our motivation is the principle of counter-pain. Admittedly I'm not aware of any scientific studies that verify it, but I am certain that it is more than simple imagination. We can only have pain in one spot. The pain is, biochemically speaking, the brain's reaction to the presence of its neurotransmitters. If multiple parts of the body send out pain signals, only the area with the greatest intensity will be examined. And therein lies the problem: the intensity. It must be high, very high.
The number and type of potential injuries reported by others is shocking. They include breaking their own nose, or shattering their sink with their head. Broken toes or head lacerations from "encountering" other objects. From the bathroom mirror to the car park wall, there is a long list. Whatever was in front of the person at the wrong time. Some have even pulled out their own teeth.
Personally, I know the urge to slam your head into the nearest wall, but I have long been able to control myself, thankfully! I have stuck to punching walls, tables, and furniture. Tables tend to be very stable, kitchen cabinets not so much. They can easily be damaged by the human fist. Unfortunately, the hand hurts for days after that. Walls, of course, are among the most unwavering and patient of objects, based on the layer of blood stains. The knuckles can still leave imprints on the plaster, however.
Sound gruesome?
It was.
But there is some good news: it's all behind me!

Now that I have oxygen and triptans at my disposal, I have not had any such impulses as the result of an attack.

How Does It Feel The Morning After?

Someone who is sick waits until they are healthy again. But someone who is chronically ill has to divorce themselves from this hope. At some point I could no longer imagine how to even lead a normal life.
Because of the spasmodic course of my disease, I am continuously faced with symptom-free - or at least nearly symptom-free - periods. That is fortunate. Realising this, though, is always a new challenge. After weeks or even months of one episode there is still that one first day of no pain, the first night uninterrupted by the stampede in my head. It's hard to describe, this moment, because many thoughts and emotions are stirred up at once. On the one hand it's unbelievably soothing, even euphoric. On the other hand I have all too often had to mourn the passing of a short spell of relief.
Still, I have not been able to build up a reliable gut feeling in all these years. This would also render a fundamental element of cluster headache ineffective, because I never know how I will feel in half an hour. This typically places me in a conundrum. My body enjoys the period of relief, and urgently needs it. My head wonders how deceptive the peace will be this time. It takes some discipline not to fall into lethargy and to simply wait until next time.
Pending this discipline, there is also the question of what I will actually do with my earned freedom. I used to try catching up on lost time and primarily tending to work I had fallen behind on. Or rather, I would attempt to do so. There was always far more left unfinished than I could hope to catch up on. It's a Sisyphean task. The attempt at breaking down pressure and emotional stress in this way usually did not work. Now I try very hard to adhere to a clear system of priorities.

At the top of the list is logistics. It's important to always have enough medication and oxygen bottles at home. As a result, it's necessary to separate tasks that can be postponed from those that can't. Some things become more complicated if they're set aside, and others just gather dust. Bills should be paid on time, but windows can be cleaned later.

It's also important to stimulate the soul. This step cannot be put down in numbers, so it's hard to find the right balance. I indulge in an even combination of leisure and movement without any guilt. And I can tell that I feel better following that formula, even though this behaviour almost certainly prevents any financial success. For me, the rungs on the career ladder are simply too far apart. Thankfully money does not make one happy, just calms one down a bit.

At some point, the first painless day was followed by the first painless week. I could always prepare for it, because an episode would never suddenly end, but rather ring out gradually. From multiple attacks per day to one attack per day. Then every other day, every third day, and then one per week. Even less and I no longer consider it to be an episode, and it doesn't happen very often. But that's not to say it never happens.

At that point the plan is fairly simple, in principle anyway. Return to normalcy! Of course, that sounds much easier than it is. My notes in the headache journal help here as well, and it is especially clear - especially in the visual pain scale - that the number of attacks continues to decrease. I know from experience how unlikely it is that the number of attacks will suddenly begin to rise.

Over?

It's not over, it's just taking a break.

 This sword of Damocles is constantly suspended over me. Even if I haven't had any attacks in months. The next attack will come for sure. This certainty is even stronger than the certainty that the next pain-free day will come, too.

The constant anxiety over the next attack is a reliable companion, and the reactions to this first attack (contrary to those upon the first pain-free day) are entirely automatic. The first is followed by the second. They occur in quickening succession and become more intense. One single attack can cause the entire house of cards to collapse. Now my energy is spent trying to maintain normalcy and react objectively. If I knew exactly when things would go downhill, it'd be easier. Unfortunately I don't, and in all these years I have not been able to develop a sense of it. I only know that it's usually not during an attack. I cannot guess how many there will be this time and how severe it will be. Objectively this means specifically looking over medication reserves and refilling when necessary.

In the meantime I have had a number of good experiences upon ingesting high doses of Verapamil. It does have its negative side-effects, but it appears effective at reducing the number of attacks and alleviating their intensity. It is and remains a feeling because I can never really know how this episode would run its course without preventative medication. In any case, this feeling is very clear.

If it's important to return to normalcy after an episode, I consider it prudent to make a planned departure from this normalcy at the beginning of another one. I avoid taking on tasks and obligations that I may not be able to stick with. I even minimise the number of appointments in my personal life. Complete social withdrawal is not good, and any doctor, therapist, and psychiatrist would confirm this. But this withdrawal is temporary, and in that time I abstain from planned appointments and dates. I don't buy any tickets to a concert a few weeks from now, for example. The entire time I'd be encumbered by the stress brought on by the question of whether I will be feeling good enough that evening. I consider this avoidance necessary. My close social circle has come to understand the process. I don't know if they all understand it, but they accept it without complaint, and I'll come along the next time.

What weigh down on me far more are the times when the pain decides to make a reappearance, especially at those exact moments when I needed it the least. Always at a time when I thought I had regained my stability in life. Be it from a professional perspective or a romantic one with a partner who made me feel safe. Numerous times I have thought that it was as though the cluster was waiting until that precise moment to re-exert its negative influence on my life. That probably sounds paranoid, but it's the impression I've had. Or rather, it's the impression I used to have, because every time I get better at working around it. It will never be nice and simple, but I won't let it have such an impact on me anymore.

Answers

I have not been successful at finding an answer to all questions, but I have been for far more than I originally expected.

If we are no longer able to change a situation, we are required to change ourselves.
Viktor Emil Frankl

Logistics of a Chronic Illness

Sometimes things happen fast. During a cluster attack, "sometimes" definitively means "always". The reaction speed when taking preventative steps is immensely important. Every minute spent waiting means another minute of having to endure the pain. Anyone who has blacked out from pain is not prepared to discuss, but calculates every second. Smooth logistics in the supply of medication is an absolute necessity.

I receive the prescriptions I need from my specialist and, in an emergency, from my doctor. Prepaid envelopes are covered by my specialist, so I can request prescriptions by phone or e-mail when required.

My pharmacy is open from 8 a.m. to 8 p.m. six days per week, and receives deliveries three times per day.

I receive the oxygen from a local medical store. I can pick it up there, but it is also delivered upon request, and on the weekend there is an emergency service and an oxygen reserve in the basement.

I cannot wait for any of this. Everything must function smoothly. I have sought out my partners and been nice to them so that they will also be nice to me. It's not very hard. A little smile, a Happy Easter and a Merry Christmas will suffice. Then it happens that one is approached by the pharmacy staff: "I knew you were coming today when I saw the Imigran on the order list." Anonymity isn't worth it here.

The most astonishing result of this tactic was when the medical store employee recognised my car when I pulled up to the parking lot. When I entered the shop, she had already brought out the oxygen bottle I had ordered over the phone.

Adjusted reserves in my own home and at any other strategic points also help with an uninterrupted, stress-free supply, of course. Reserves of the reserves can also be kept at work or with (nearby) relatives simply so that one is not suddenly left without a safety blanket.

I personally keep a store of acute medication - Imigran inject, Zomig nasal, and oxygen bottles - at home in quantities that will roughly last for one of my bad weeks. Everybody needs different amounts. This could be two small, 2-litre oxygen bottles or five large, 10-litre ones.
Unlike the common phobias of darkness, spiders, or flying, the fear of being without the medication that saves me is very well-justified. No method of confrontation commonly used in behavioral therapy can help against this anxiety. Much like how a skydiver securely checks their equipment, the cluster headache patient should pay attention to their emergency reserves. It's worth the effort. Those who neglect to do so will only punish themselves in the end.

Headache Journal

In his classic of motivational literature *How to Stop Worrying and Start Living*, Dale Carnegie recommends physically writing down problems, fears, worries, and possible solutions. Every doctor suggests that pain patients keep a journal. And all I can say is, follow this advice!
Keeping a journal serves to sort one's thoughts and helps correctly reconstruct sequences of events. A pain journal in particular helps document pain as quantitatively as possible. The intensity of pain cannot be measured in the same way a kilo of flour is. A properly maintained headache journal, however, gives the patient, their attending physician, and any advisors an objective overview of the sequence of pain.
You will certainly stop keeping track of whether you have been torn out of your sleep by the pain three times per night for two or three months. Such a trend can only give you the hope you urgently need, or indicate the remaining effectiveness of a medication - an effectiveness that may otherwise not enter into your consciousness at all, thereby becoming a wasted opportunity. That would be fatal.

You do not feel noticeably better when you only have two attacks at night instead of three. You also don't feel better when it's just one. You only become consciously aware of something once you have been able to sleep through three nights once more. At the very least, I also find the interim objectives worthwhile.

In my headache journal it was the Zomig nasal that had a positive effect. After the first dozen uses I was able to notice that, in most cases, I had a break period of at least twelve hours after each use. One time it only lasted for eleven, and in another instance the Zomig nasal sadly didn't have any effect at all. But it gave me ten half-days of freedom from pain.

It sounds long enough for someone to be able to become consciously aware of it. But I couldn't. I did not perceive this actually significant improvement as such. Thankfully the more frequent and longer breaks from the pain still ended up in my headache journal.

This resulted in a very simple change to my behaviour. When I had taken Zomig, I felt far more secure. In the hours following I had room for all sorts of activities, from daily errands like shopping at the supermarket, to a mindful walk or a ride on my bicycle - I could leave the house whenever I wanted, keep up with social contacts, move around, and exercise.

Even though it can't be proven empirically, I am very sure that this simple state of affairs that palpably accelerated further recovery or the continued abatement of the episode.

This is why I believe that keeping a headache journal is an elementary and extremely crucial part of dealing with cluster headache. One of the main reasons being that it doesn't cost a thing and is free of side-effects. Those who say it is too much trouble keeping a headache journal are either irredeemably ignorant or their pains are simply not severe enough. That's all there is to say about the matter that a journal should be kept. The second step puts forth the question of how.

Sadly, none of the pain journals I know are suitable for cluster headache patients. The problem here, as with other trigeminal autonomic cephalalgias, lies in the relatively short - and all the more frequent - pain intervals. The pain scenario must thus not be recorded by the day, as it is actually more sensible to scale it by hours. What I recommend, and what I do, is documenting the beginning of the attack, its duration, its intensity (pain severity on a scale of 0 to 10), and the medication used.

How the respective sufferer actually does it will also depend on their personal preferences. Some go for the classic pen and paper. I prefer to do it electronically, and I keep a headache journal in the form of a table in a spreadsheet. Each sheet corresponds to one week. With the current layout, six pain events can be recorded per day. A field is also open for any freely formulated comments. The advantage of this layout for me is that trends become clear simply by flipping through the sheets. More attacks mean more entries, and - at least in my case - more extensive comments.

I have also expanded my electronic headache journal with a visual pain severity analysis. The duration of the respective attack is multiplied by the intensity of the pain, and then the individual results are added up. The results may be shown by day or by week, and in my experience they very clearly show the wave-like sequence of a cluster episode.

An online headache journal and a headache journal app would also be in line with the times. But before anyone can even say the words "privacy policy", I would like to push the topic a bit further into the future. I am not currently aware of any proper solution, and it would not be of any additional benefit to the sufferer. Anyone with a pen and paper can continue to use it for many years to come. Those with a PC or Mac at home can integrate my headache journal template into a spreadsheet.

My template can be found online at:
www.schmerzfrisstseele.de/kopfschmerztagebuch/

Severe Disability

The term "cluster headache" entered into my life one night in December 2004 as I was searching online for the phrases "headache" and "inability to work". Over the years I have since continued to learn how to deal with my disease, but there are still too many periods when I am not able to work. So does that make me disabled, or not?
Disability is defined as a long-term and serious impairment of a person to participate and/or get involved in society and the workplace. I believe I have very clearly met this criterion. But in Germany, one is only officially disabled when they own a disabled person's pass with a disability level (DL) of 50 or more.
Anyone hoping to obtain a disabled person's pass must apply at the regional pension office or the office for social affairs. First the right office has to be found, which depends on the applicant's town and state. Upon entering a town and the key phrase "pension office", the internet will spit out the right place. Those living in the country may have to enter the name of the nearest city.
The respective office provides the application as a pre-printed form (also often available online). The official name of this form is "First-Time Application as per § 69 of the Ninth Volume of the Social Code (SGB IX) to Determine a Disability and to Issue a Pass". The office then examines it and ascertains the level of disability. To this end, the applicant must provide the office with any available medical records. If an applicant lost their eyesight or both legs as a result of an accident, then a very clear determination is likely. But if they have rarely been to the doctor and were never on sick leave, then the process will probably result in rejection.
My first application was also rejected. Now it's possible to appeal that decision, resulting in a reassessment. Applicants can now expect to be invited to see the medical officer or independent medical examiner. After my appeal, I was assigned a DL of 40. Experience shows that a first-

time application for a disease that cannot be classified by high-tech medicine, like cluster headache, is very often rejected and filing for an appeal is the norm.

I had decided to accept my assigned DL of 40, and to file a change request after the next pain episode. This application was also rejected, so then I had to submit an appeal once more. In practice, such an appeal is no more than a comprehensive letter in which I disclosed my situation. This time my appeal, too, was turned down. The next step is filing a complaint at the local social welfare court. It sounds dramatic, but this is also merely an extensive letter that must, of course, be formulated correctly. The case is ten reexamined by another office. In my case, acknowledgment of a DL of 80 was recommended a few weeks after I filed my complaint. With no court proceedings. I agreed to it and was able to receive my disabled person's pass a few days later.

The pass serves as proof of the acceptance of rights and disadvantage benefits legally afforded to people with a disability. This includes special protection against termination of employment, a claim to additional leave, and income tax benefits. Based on my experience, a disabled person's pass is first issued only for a certain amount of time.

Essentially, the most detailed documentation of the disease possible is helpful. I assume that my headache journals and the fact that I am a patient of the distinguished headache specialist Dr. Astrid Gendolla certainly didn't hurt the granting of my disabled person's pass.

If the first round doesn't work, you cannot despair and should firmly take the next step. A little endurance never hurts. In my case, however, when all was said and done I had only filled out two applications and three lengthy letters, two appeals, and one complaint.

But does it also make sense to embarrass yourself with this pass? To officially brand yourself as disabled? I know of other people who have a fundamental problem with accepting themselves as such. I didn't have this issue. It had been clear to me for years that I was no longer fully capable, and thus not indefinitely employable. It was obvious that my professional future would require all my cards on the table, and this includes the official designation as disabled. But everyone must weigh the pros and cons for themselves.

In retrospect, I'm also happy I took this step. The official disability status makes it easier to discuss the severity of the disease sometimes. The pass shows that it's not just the same kind of headaches that everyone else gets. The disabled person's pass is not issued indiscriminately, and so even possessing one carries a certain validation, and saves any unnecessary explanations.

I'm Getting by, Right?

Perhaps I should say I've learned to compose myself. I am certainly leading an alternative version of my life. Plan B or C. But is it right to denigrate that?

Allow me to use a radical example: someone in a wheelchair cannot play football or ride their bike or go skiing. That's clear to everyone, including the wheelchair-bound person themselves. They can use clear criteria to determine whether that life is still worth living for them. Some have the unwavering optimism and joie de vivre of a Florian Sitzmann (disabled athlete and author), and others are shattered by their fate. Others break down even though there has been no fate for them to face. These examples illustrate that it's not about the situation, but the value that it presents to us.

The awareness of this rather simple fact has made a long-lasting impression on my life. I am no saint (just an angel, but that's another story). I am also not always able to pass through my life with a positive attitude. There are days - many days, even - when I don't feel well because I'm in constant pain and I have not been able to enjoy one restful night in weeks. And in that position it is easy, very easy, to keep whining. Whining that I'm alone, that I don't have a (well-paying) job, that I have it worse than everyone else, and so on, and so on, and so on.

But the only person I'm upsetting is myself. And very little will improve because of my complaining. I may inspire pity among people I know, and that is the last thing that I want. "Poor little thing." No - please, not that!

I may not always be able to whistle a happy little tune, but trying to whenever possible makes my life palpably better. If I had a patented recipe for how that works, I would give it away in an instant. But I can list the autosuggestive methods I regularly follow to improve my mood.

First, an experiment in the other direction. We need an open space of about five metres. Stand there, more slouched than upright. Let your head and shoulders hang. Drag your feet and shuffle and slide right across the room. How do you feel? Before turning back, straighten yourself up, hold your head high and your neck elongated. Now bounce with your knees and walk back. Was the return trip better?

There are countless motivational books and guides to happiness that contain hundreds of suggestions like that. Anyone who's inclined to do so could chant incantations into the mirror and feel better. The method isn't important in the end, as long as it works. No holds barred, although psychoactive substances are not allowed.

Those with a penchant for sarcasm, like myself, will have motivational literature in their bookshelf next to books like How to Ruin My Life - By Following a System by Rainer Sachse.

Despite all motivational training, there are still unresolved issues. And - snap! - there's that merciless optimism again. Because "still unresolved" means that the issues can be solved. Even more, it shows that there is something to look forward to. The most important of the unanswered questions is ultimately only pecuniary in nature. Will I ever find a job and an employer compatible with cluster? And will the cluster allow me to pursue regular work? Will the open spaces I frequently need ever be provided to me? What will I do if that doesn't happen? A life of basic security is not an alluring prospect, although I'm happy to live in a country that offers suitable social backup.

What if I didn't live in a Western, industrial nation, but rather in the Australian Outback or the coast of Greenland, or in the depths of the Congo? Would I be dead already, or not sick at all? I may try it out someday. Right now, I'm still too cowardly.

What if I had been more industrious and adept at saving in my younger years so that I could now go into retirement with acceptable earnings? Would I be happier? Yes, I would be. Richard David Precht says that money generally increases the number of opportunities to develop. And more important to me than development is security. Had I known sooner what is going on, I would definitely have become a civil servant. If the dog hadn't shat, it wouldn't have caught the hare. It is what it is, and the best will be made of it.

Enjoy Life

My life has included long periods with very few positive thoughts, and with love only as a painful memory. I had forgotten that I alone am responsible for how I feel. Nobody else.

What does self-responsibility mean?

Each of us must always decide whether to act or not, whether to continue indulging a habit or not. This responsibility is not something we can avoid or postpone. If we abstain from consciously facing these things and their consequences, all we are doing is limiting our number of opportunities. By ignoring our opportunities, we are unconsciously making a decision. And doing nothing can be the most fateful decision of all.

My solution: get out of the box! Or even better, get rid of it!

One hundred years ago Sybil F. Partridge came out with Just for Today, ten prompts to help one take small steps to get out of their shell. I would like to briefly describe the three best:

- Just for today, I will take care of my Body. I will exercise it, care for it, and nourish it, and not abuse it nor neglect it; so that it will be a perfect machine for my will.
- Just for Today, I will be agreeable. I will look as well as I can, dress as becomingly as possible, talk low, act courteously, be liberal with flattery, criticize not one bit nor find fault with anything, and not try to regulate nor improve anybody.
- Just for today, I will try to live through this day only, and not tackle my whole life-problem at once.

I cannot promise anybody that this will help. But it is certain that tomorrow need not be like yesterday. And that it is worth not sticking your head in the sand.

Even if it rains today, the sun can shine again tomorrow. Only very few people will refute that. So why do we often go about our lives with so little optimism? We only have one life, and we should care for and cherish it.

If it's raining cats and dogs for a week, the hope for a sunny day may dissipate somewhat, but nobody will seriously believe that the sun has disappeared forever. If it's really coming down like buckets so that rivers breach and harvests are destroyed, then it's understandable to be furious at the ineffable weather. And yet even then, nobody will think that the sun is gone, even though it's long been hidden behind a thick blanket of clouds.

There comes a day when it makes a reappearance and its warm rays reach us again. This doesn't necessarily mean that everything is simply over and we can carry on like before. Depending on the extent of the storm and the scope of the damage, comprehensive (clean-up) work may be required.

Not much is different in our lives. Some may be born with a silver spoon in their mouth and will never have to trudge through the darkness. Many of us have to deal with adversity from time to time. Unlike the sun, which we always believe in deep down, it happens that we lose faith in ourselves. But for as long as we are here, there is a new tomorrow every day. And every new day does not have to be like the last one. Even a hundred failed attempts do not mean that the next will not work out. Doing nothing, stagnating, is ultimately its own decision, perhaps not a conscious one but definitely the worst.

If I am looking for a job and have been rejected for months or even years, it's definitely frustrating and gruelling. But if I take from it that there is no meaning to anything and stop writing applications altogether, then once again it is me who is taking the opportunity away.

Of course it's difficult to find the motivation to keep going. It's hard to consider why previous strategies have not been successful and what could be done differently, and hopefully better. One plan for this may be to find a way to benefit from the lack of prospects. If I think my application probably won't be successful, I can bet on the risk and simply try using unconventional methods - stick out from the group of other applicants by being noticeable. This is not an endorsement for boorishness, but rather creativity. However, it is worth ensuring that faulty endeavours are not repeated. If I have not received any acceptances or rejections of applications for months, another form is necessary.

If my doctor cannot help any further because they lack the required specialisation, then it's necessary to find a specialist. Unfortunately, doctors are hard-pressed to admit that they don't know anything else and their treatment is nothing more than stabs in the dark. This is the cue to use your own self-responsibility to make the necessary changes. Others will hardly ever do this for us, and are also not able.

It took me five years to find a doctor to diagnose my cluster headache syndrome. Even worse! I was able to diagnose myself with it at some point. This in turn allowed me to find a specialist who confirmed my self-diagnosis. In that time I have avoided all medical professionals a number of times and declared them incapable. Not one of them was able to help. I did not stumble across the right doctor on my own, of course. It was bad luck, plain and simple. Now I know from other sufferers that some of them had the same experience. Others were more fortunate. They found the right doctor who knew the disease.
Had I kept my head in the sand back then, I may still not have received a diagnosis, let alone any medication and helpful treatments. The mere thought sends chills down my spine.

A good seven years have passed since the diagnosis, and in that time I have adapted to new medications, or new medications came onto the market and needed test subjects. Seven years in which I have worked against the systems with general management strategies, sometimes with more luck and others with less. Now I spend my seeming half-life as a chronically ill person. It includes concrete outage periods caused by pain, but also maintenance of the logistics. Regular guests at doctors' offices, pharmacies, and medical stores will do themselves a favour by becoming well-known there.
Of course, none of that is nice and it's not fun, but it's necessary to keep the other half of my life exactly that: a life. That is far more than I expected, and it's ultimately worth the effort. Admittedly, it takes a while to be able to internally accept the time used on it, but the impressive logic doesn't change. I have to invest half my life in managing a disease merely so that I can keep the other half for myself.
That's not very compatible with today's society of performance, but nevertheless there is a "tomorrow" that I

did not believe in "yesterday". Even if I didn't know where life was heading or why, I did not give up, and now I can say that it has been worthwhile. Those who do nothing will receive nothing in return. Those who wait for something to pass can wait a very, very long time.

And nobody has to be embarrassed if they aren't immediately able to implement these strategies. For me, the process has taken twelve years, and it's not complete. For one, I have to continuously motivate myself, and I'm not able to do that every day. Plus there is always something new to learn. Nothing is perfect and everything can be improved. But only someone who makes mistakes can become better.

When I write that I invest half my life in managing a disease, I would like to specify one certain aspect of that. Because this management also entails intensive work on the part of me that is not sick at all, and which wants to be empowered.

There are diseases that are just there and cannot be conjured away. In this regard, it only makes sense to put a lot of energy into what remains in order to make it possible for the sufferer to tackle their personal issues.

To be more specific, yoga is not the silver bullet against actual pain. But it really gives me an entirely new way to address it. This in turn helps immensely. If I may get to the point, it hurts as much as ever, but I can cope with it better. It's not a cure-all by any means, as there can be no such thing. However, I am now firmly convinced that it's worth it to find your own solution.

Do more of what makes you happy!

Velosophy

The wheel is, without a doubt, one of the greatest of mankind's inventions. It may even be the greatest. On top of that, may I add, it has never had any negative side-effects.

A simple bicycle can be so much more. It allows for relatively broad mobility with few resources. It provides the rider with a connection to their surroundings without overwhelming the senses. And it lets the rider participate in a highly technological world with very primitive means. It rolls swiftly through urban areas without the congestion assistance of navigational devices. And it always finds a parking spot in the immediate vicinity of the destination without a parking assistant or reverse camera.

All one has to do is breathe and pedal.

Here I would like to digress a little and mention two types of behaviour that, in my own experience, are difficult for many other people to accept.

One: using a bike every day.
Two: rolling one's own cigarettes.

When smokers stand together, a self-roller is almost always patronisingly offered a filtered cigarette. It seems to me that the smoker of filtered cigarettes wants to indulge the poor self-roller a bit. But they, in turn, don't want something ready-made, with or without a filter. They understand the rolling of cigarettes as a preparatory ritual and want to keep it that way. Other countries, other customs? To call this phenomenon typically German may be a step too far, but I would bet that this phenomenon does not exist in the Netherlands, where the rolling population is much higher.

Riding a bike is similar. If a cyclist comes upon a birthday party, somebody will almost certainly offer to drive them home later. Riders of racing cycles may avoid judgment, but regular cyclists are suspicious, especially those who ride a bike with a basket to the grocery store. "With a bike? No driving licence?" Words like those are always floating around the room. I will explain here once and for all that no, none of it has anything to do with some sort of ordeal or a lost driving licence, but rather it has everything to do with quality of living. I would prefer not to sit in a tin box more often than I have to.

Other countries, other customs? In the Netherlands, the bicycle is socially accepted. And I am beginning to understand why I have always felt so comfortable among our neighbours.

Alex Rühle once phrased it like so in a blog article about cycling in winter for the newspaper Süddeutsche Zeitung:

"The few times when I have taken the bus or streetcar to work in the wintertime, I later felt as though I had spent the night in an old sock drawer. The stagnant air, the chipped windows, the endlessly bleak aisle, and most people on the streetcar look so crumpled up, as though they had been presented with a certificate of discharge from existence before boarding. Smile a little, people! Sing a song! But no, they jerk and jolt their way to their destination in silence."

And he is absolutely right when he writes, "Pedal, breathe, look, relax, contemplate. Nowhere do things seem better than they do on a bike."

This leads from the general revelation as to why cycling is both economically and ecologically sensible to the fact cycling personally helps me as a cluster headache patient.

Put quite simply, sitting on a bike means moving. Out in the open air. In essence, it's the fundamental programme behind every psychotherapeutic measure. Light and motion always have a positive effect on us, and have no harmful side-effects.

Furthermore, the bicycle helps reduce irritants for me. In times when I have not been able to sleep enough for weeks because of constant nightly attacks, the entire world seemed to pass by me too quickly. During times like these I am extremely averse to driving cars, as I am not really able to take in all of the information around me. With my bike, I can travel longer distances than my feet will carry me. I am thus able to move as much as my momentary sensory capacities allow. With my bike, I can ride as slowly as I like without provoking a choir of horns in my wake. And if traffic is too hectic for me to cross the street, there's no harm in riding up to a pedestrian crosswalk and crossing during the next green light.

This may sound a little like kindergarten. But when you're alone and it looks like you're seeing the world around you through a big cotton ball, then the bicycle guarantees mobility. The bike is as necessary as a wheelchair for a paraplegic, or an assistance dog for the blind.

Pedaling, breathing, and relaxing are also easiest when I'm on a bike. Just like pedaling, breathing, and contemplating. A great number of ideas and insight have come to me on my bike. I have to rely on oxygen. Pedal, breathe, and enjoy. For me it's simply the full wellness package.

In my own experience, a better condition helps with overcoming the next episode. Not just the condition either, but also ensuring phases of respite and working with limitations. A quick ride to the bakery isn't enough. But the Ruhr Region has more than enough hills to break a sweat. Anyone who has trained enough here will not find any alpine terrain further south in Wuppertal or Hagen, but rather many other challenges.

The process of cresting a slope is similar to a headache attack. I find it very helpful to train for this process over and over, and especially to be certain that, just as every mountain has a summit, every attack has an end.

On her "Lovely Bicycle!" blog, writer *Velouria* published a wonderful text on these thoughts that shoot through a cyclist's head while scaling a mountain. These thoughts have a lot in common with how one should deal with a disease - even if one loses their breath halfway through!

Her text can be found on the "Lovely Bicycle!" blog:
http://lovelybike.blogspot.de/2012/08/the-12-stages-of-uphill-addiction.html

Outlooks

What are the current prospects for new medication and treatments? The short answer, unfortunately, is: "Nothing specific." To be prosaic, there are too few of us. The number of patients is too small for the pharma industry to take particular interest in cluster headache sufferers. The available medication is either also approved to treat cluster headache or is used off-label. There is no medication designed specifically to treat cluster headache. All triptans are primarily conceived to treat migraine. Thankfully, someone noticed that they also have an effect on cluster headache. Nevertheless the usage of Imigran and others is a by-product.

Yet there is a relatively specific assumption of the way it works. For preventative medication, like Verapamil, such estimations are stabs in the dark. Only observation is possible. Of course, I also like to take a medication that I know to be helpful, even if nobody knows how exactly it works. Still, the discovery of new medication is left entirely to chance.

The effectiveness of new medication must be verified in clinical trials. Their harmlessness and the risk-benefit ratio must also be determined. Generally the trial in question is a phase III study in order to verify the effectiveness of a therapeutic measure (like a medicine, for example). And this is only the last step of medicine approval. These procedures are very comprehensive, and thus costly. Because the pharmaceutical corporations are companies that want and need to make money, the targeted development of new or better medication to counter cluster headache is not exactly high on their list of priorities. And if they want to develop a medication, it would be very helpful if the working mechanism of cluster headache was known. But it is not. There is research being done in this area, but not nearly with the same intensity dedicated to other diseases.

In my experience, new and better medications are not impossible, but at least unlikely. Waiting or hoping for them doesn't seem like something I can recommend. Anyone who goes through life with their eyes and ears open will always hear about research and new insight into diseases like dementia or Parkinson's, and there are indeed studies about cluster headache. Yet they are more for taking stock, and are miles away from presenting new solution-based approaches. Because there have been no new approaches to treating the much more intensively researched dementia-related diseases, I will be so bold as to deduce that, for the time being, any progress in the treatment of cluster headache can only be expected as a result of chance.

There are attempts to overcome the pain attacks via so-called deep brain stimulation. This entails the surgical implantation of electrodes in the brain that aim to correct disease-induced errors. This method is primarily used in the treatment of Parkinson's. The clinical trial also tests this method against cluster headache, epilepsy, depression, and Tourette's syndrome. it is very certainly a personalised attempt at treatment that can be discussed as a last resort for patients who are not responding to any other treatments. In some cases, epilepsy patients even have the opportunity to undergo neurosurgery to remove parts of the brain. It is a very risky operation, but it has been proven to prevent attacks.

Similar success with deep brain stimulation (DBS) to treat cluster headache is currently a topic of debate. This also applies to other experimental surgical procedures like spinal cord stimulation (SCS), pterygopalatine ganglion stimulation (PPG-S/PPG-I/PPG radio frequency stimulation), and occipital nerve stimulation (ONS). All of these ultimately aim to have a positive influence on the patient's pain via the electrical stimulation of various nerves.

Transcutaneous vagus nerve stimulation (tVNS), which does not involve surgery but also works with electrical stimuli, is gentler.

In my personal opinion it is more a desperate stab in the dark than targeted treatment. It is called "experimental treatment" because that is exactly what it is. For me, such a thing is out of the question even given all of the pressure exerted by recurring pain. But I am also not resistant to treatment.

Another stimulation method, namely that of the sphenopalatine ganglion (SPG), seems a little better. I think it's really nice that this approach is not a secondary or tertiary assessment of a method. SPG came about as an idea from a research group at an American university. A spin-off company established as a result now sells the stimulators. The idea is based on the assumption that this sphenopalatine ganglion also plays a central role in the perception and transmission of pain as a nerve fibre. Stimulation strives to impede this role, thereby improving the pain situation. There is a certain sense to this logic in my eyes, and the operation is not as drastic as that required for deep brain stimulation. Initial studies inspire hope. However, it is still too early to be able to form a conclusive opinion.

Miscellaneous

A collection of further important points, counterpoints and supposed trifles.
Also to be understood as a collection of everyday aids.

Even from the stones placed in our path, something beautiful can be constructed.
Johann Wolfgang von Goethe

Hard Drive Receiver

There are practical, everyday things that make life with cluster headache more bearable. This includes a hard drive receiver or some other form of reception for the television. The importance of this cannot be underestimated. If every time you watch a movie you miss the middle, the ending, or even the entire broadcast, then over time it becomes much more frustrating than you would think at first. Since I have a hard drive receiver, I can at least counteract the everyday disruptive effect of cluster with the click of a button. My kingdom for the time-shift function.
During one summer episode, almost all of my attacks struck inexplicably during the mountain stages of the Tour de France. While the final ascent was being broadcast live, I couldn't even see for all the pain, but thanks to this little button on the remote control I could watch it all again once the attack subsided. For me, that's a little quality of life I have regained thanks to technology.

Rusted End Caps

Always Loosen Them in Advance!

Stupid mistakes happen. Little technical mistakes that are entirely unnecessary and superfluous.
Large bottles of oxygen have a safety cap that is screwed onto the bottle's threaded valve. When the bottle is delivered to your home, you don't know where the bottle has been. Perhaps it had been stored outside and exposed to the elements. This could result in the thread being rusted shut, or at least difficult to loosen.
Encountering such a rust-sealed cap in the middle of the night is completely unnecessary. But when the first bottle is empty, you have to replace the fitting. And, according to Murphy's Law, this is guaranteed to be in the middle of the night, and when there aren't any pliers lying next to

the bottle. And yes, for at least three years now not one cap has gotten stuck.

Of course, I also encounter such carelessness. For example, one night in autumn 2013 when I was very angry and swore that I would never allow this to happen again. Loosening the cap when the bottle arrives and then just screwing on a thread is not really asking for a whole lot.

People who really want to play it safe can also have two bottles with fittings at the ready, of course. I'm happy with one large and one small bottle. The small, portable bottle is right next to my bed at night so that I can keep the pain-induced awakening as brief as possible. Then I usually switch over to the big bottle.

And there is a question hidden in all this that nobody dares ask: of course I take the little bottle with me to the bathroom when the nightly attacks come with urinary urgency. I would also drag the big one along the tiles were it not for the stairs in my flat. So I prefer the smaller one in my backpack.

Rehabilitation or not?

In patient circles, there is no unanimity when it comes to the sense and nonsense of rehabilitative stays. By definition, they are supposed to help people recover. Naturally this can't be a cure-all, because there is no true recovery from cluster headache. If I expect that from treatment, then I will be disappointed. Yet nobody is stopping me from seeing treatment as an opportunity to recharge my own batteries. There are almost no worldly worries on site. Breakfast, lunch, and dinner are provided. There is no flat to clean, and a lot of nature in the immediate vicinity. Those who promptly contact the clinic for an informative discussion need not worry about receiving their medication, as it is just a few meters down the hall at the nursing station.

To cluster headache patients, treatment is nothing more than a trip to the spa, but it's also nothing less. Anyone who takes advantage of it can gain a lot from rehabilitation. But without active cooperation, then there will surely be no success. Ultimately, many tools are at work in every round of treatment that are also present in mind-body medicine. This is defined as medicine that helps the body strengthen its healthy areas, and it doesn't matter what disease you have. The more the patient understands the types of treatment, the more effective they are.

Yoga

Yoga is one of these tools that can help the body strengthen its healthy points. Yoga is an Indian philosophy that encompasses a broad range of mental and physical exercises. It appears that yoga has proven to have some positive effects on mental and physical health. That is the only way to explain why health insurance providers finance yoga courses as preventative measures. It helps me look inward and find peace. To restore energy.
Of course, it doesn't help to simply know that it's helpful. It's absolutely imperative that it be practised. Yoga must not be the right tool for everyone, because everyone is different. Thankfully there are many other methods with a similar objective, like qi gong, tai chi, autogenic training, progressive muscle relaxation, and meditation. Playing a certain sport or a simple walk through the woods can have a similar effect. It's really important that you don't force yourself, but rather enjoy yourself. Once again - do more of what makes you happy.
Yoga is what you make of it. And it is guaranteed not to help anyone who doesn't try it out.

Doctor Visits are a Form of Social Contact

To this day I have no idea whether it's good or bad, or maybe a sign of something else. But it happens when you go to the doctor often enough. It happens to me. Some time ago I realised that a visit to the doctor or a treatment session has become just as much a form of social contact as hanging out with friends. It makes it quite clear that I have a circle of doctors and therapists under whose care I feel safe. And this circumstance generally has a positive effect on treatment.
There have been times when I could not even imagine that. Too many clueless and disinterested doctors crossed my path during those first years of my cluster career. But now when I have an appointment with my neurologist, I have a habit of greeting her with the words, "Nice to see you." And I truly mean it.

Traditional Chinese Medicine (TCM), Homeopathy, Shamanism, Etc.

One could roughly make the following objective conclusion: the market of so-called alternative treatments has boomed in recent years, and it's become incredibly expansive. Some of the procedures can be beneficial as supplements to treatment with medication, but only a small minority of them have been scientifically tested.
Subjectively, I will take the liberty to discuss the threshold between placebo effect and charlatanry. Because faith can certainly move mountains, I don't want to denigrate or oppose any treatment. But the working mechanisms of many alternative healing methods are rather suspect in my opinion. (While doing yoga, for example, I don't chant an Om Shanti mantra.) In the case of acupuncture I can imagine that the compulsory break of at least 30 minutes is more effective than the needles themselves. But without needles you may concentrate too hard on your

surroundings, making the needles necessary. I really don't care at all if they touch a meridian or not.

Means and methods that a responsible medical practitioner would not stand behind are no longer debatable. Yet desperate people tend to consider the impossible as well. For example, I have heard reports of the usage of snake poison. Unfortunately there are unethical people who see dollar signs when they look at a desperate patient and fuel the slightest bit of hope in them. All forms of treatment must be discussed with your doctor, for your own sake.

Holding On

People need physical contact. But this also means being able to hold onto something. I lost count of the hours that I spent sitting apathetically in the pale glow of the television when I did not immediately fall back asleep after an attack in the night. It's a double-edged sword. When I forget my lack of pain as a desperate wish because of unfulfillment, then I usually miss the chance to find balance. I miss the warmth of a person who serves as a harbour for the soul. Curiously, however, I feel the loneliness even more distinctly when the pain subsides.

Traumatisation

I believe that I have been traumatised, and from what I have seen so are most other sufferers.

According to Wikipedia, trauma is a psychological injury evoked by strong mental disturbance stemming from a traumatic experience. Potentially traumatic events may include natural disasters, a hostage situation, rape, or accidents with drastically serious consequences. Such incidents can trigger extreme stress in a person along with feelings of helplessness or horror, and may permanently alter their own self-perception and worldview.

It is also revealed that normal cognitive processes in the brain can be impaired by trauma, resulting in the formation of mental symptoms. These symptom patterns are largely independent from whether the patient's trauma was triggered by acts of war, natural disasters, or some other traumatic incident. This tells me that my complete artwork could become much larger if I don't pay attention. This is where I feel the principle of mind-body medicine becomes important for strengthening the healthy parts of the body. I cannot say it often enough: "Do more of what makes you happy."

One of my favourite sentences in the definition of trauma is, "For many people, these symptoms recede some time after the traumatic event." One dare not speak of recurring traumatic incidents. However, mine come back, and they will always come back. No matter what and how much I do. I will never be able to prevent my pain attacks from coming home. And I cannot blame anybody for it. All I would be doing in the end is torturing myself.

However, it does provide slight consolation that the correlation between chronic pain and associated trauma is becoming increasingly visible at the professional level. This will most likely not change the state of affairs, but at least it will be taken seriously.

The trauma experienced by chronic pain patients was a topic at the 2010 German Pain Congress in Mannheim. Research conducted by Christian Sorg and Valentin Riedl at the Rechts der Isar Hospital of the Technical University of Munich proved corresponding changes in the brain. These show that a state of calm for a chronic pain patient is not that at all.

Smoking

The English Wikipedia article on cluster headache cites a report from Markus Schürks and Hans-Christoph Diener with the title "Cluster headache and lifestyle habits": "Nicotine can trigger cluster headache attacks and the disease often occurs in individuals with a high dependence on nicotine. In some cases passive smoking may trigger cluster headache pain. However, it is unclear whether there is a causal relationship between smoking and cluster headache. Some researchers believe that people suffering from cluster headache have a predisposition for certain characteristics, like smoking or other lifestyle habits."
Nonsense! We just don't stop smoking because cigarettes acutely alleviate the pain. If heroin helped, the percentage of addicts among clusterheads would be high.

Time

I have gotten used to having time. I show up so promptly to appointments that I am never hounded. At least I try to. And every time I'm not able, I can sense how well I'm doing at behaving that way. The only way to have time is to take time.

Minimising Irritants

I always feel that it's counterproductive when I expose myself to a broad range of stimuli. One example of this could be the bustle of a room filled with people. The greater the lengths I go to avoid any sort of chaos, the better. And yes, I have thought about living in a monastery a number of times.

FAQ - Frequently Asked Questions

I would like to use the following pages to respond to questions, comments, and key words that I frequently encountered as reactions to this book. As long as new, interesting questions reach me and people are interested in this book, this chapter will continue to be expanded with each new edition. That's the plan, anyway!

"Why did you start writing this book?"

The reason was pure desperation and bitterness. I had the feeling that nobody understands how poorly I am doing. I also felt that nobody could listen to or help me.
Thankfully I have found suitable translators in the meantime. Otherwise it would have become a sad book that would not have been able to help anybody. And, even worse, I would still be leading a sad life.

"Which phobia do you share with Mareile Kurtz?"

That's in her book. But to be clear, I share the phobia with her and not with anybody else. This narrows down the possibilities to exactly one phobia in particular.

"You're so brave! You reveal so much about yourself."

I didn't see it that way, nor did I intend it to be so. While the book was coming together over the years, I never had these thoughts. At first it was a cry of desperation. Then it flowed smoothly into a mixture of biography, self-reflection, and guidebook. "Maybe I can help others, show them shortcuts. If I'm able to inspire only one person, then my mission has been fulfilled."
Thoughts like those are the only ones that I harboured. I never thought it brave of me to grant the public insight into very intimate aspects of my life. Throughout discussions in single and group therapy I noticed the necessity of it. Because nobody can help me with secrets that I keep to myself. Nobody can now HOW badly I'm doing if I keep my condition bottled up. By making such a revelation, I'm definitely doing myself a favour.
I don't know if it's brave to reveal something about yourself. Based on my own, personal system of values, it's not. But I have also come to know that nobody exploits it. Even before this book I had told some people how I'm doing. First doctors, therapists, fellow patients, fellow sufferers. Later on I told friends and my family. And now, with this book, an exponential number of strangers. And to this day nobody has had an uncomfortable reaction to me revealing so much about myself.

«Should people say, 'Get well soon'?»

The short answer: "Rather not." Among ourselves, we wish each other times without pain.
The long answer is a philosophical discourse shaped by personal manifestation as well as special consideration of the point in time along the personal escalation curve. Sound kind of complicated? That's because it is. But it can be summarised more comprehensively.

For one, clusterheads are either chronic or episodic. The episodics have remission phases, breaks you could say. Periods of months, sometimes even years, without pain attacks. The pain phases, referred to as episodes, always follow a curve, at least for me. It starts with an attack. It could easily be two weeks until the next one. Then I only have one week, and then the following week there are two attacks. Worst-case scenario I ultimately end up having nights when there is no keeping track of the exact number of attacks. Because it's been burned into my brain that such an episode can last for three, but also even eighteen months, I don't want to hear the words, "Get well soon," at the beginning of an episode. However, toward the end of an episode I am happy to accept such kind words. Obviously I don't have some cluster meter on my forehead that instantly shows everyone where exactly I am at that moment. "Get well soon" thus remains a minefield.

It's even worse, and yet all the more clear, for chronic sufferers. They have no remission phases and are thus constantly experiencing pain attacks. So here, one could ask themselves if they would wish a diabetic, "Get well soon," and then draw their own conclusions.

But because this is all invisible to everyone else, I pledge to respond o these words with a simple thank-you.

"How appropriate are expressions of pity?"

Not at all, plain and simple.
Compassion? Sure!
Pity? No!

"Estimate - how many sufferers are there?"

Common or uncommon, that's the question here. There are figures on the prevalence (disease frequency) of cluster headache. Widely varying figures.
So I would like to withhold any quantitative estimates because I'm not sure how many patients there actually are. Nobody knows how many there are. What I do know, however, is that I often hear the phrase, "I actually know somebody..." in conversation. There are people whose quality of living is suffering because of pain. From time to time. And then with breaks. Just like with cluster headache. It takes a while before you go to the doctor. Then whenever you're sitting there, you're doing well. I think that there is a considerable estimate. But I also believe that many of those patients included in this estimate don't have a severe manifestation. At least to the extent that they are able to handle it. I spoke with patients who, in 15 years, had never had an attack that lasted longer than 15 minutes. I have no verification and it's my entirely personal opinion, but I think that the number of cluster headache sufferers is much higher than is generally assumed. A large number of them thankfully just have a much milder manifestation.

"Have you since been able to answer the question, 'Why me'? Or do you no longer want an answer to that?"

There is no rational, sensible, or helpful answer to this question. So I have stopped asking myself. As I described in the chapter dedicated to it, desperation will drive people into the trap of this question. There's a fatal aspect to it, as the answer cannot be found.
It's a vicious cycle!
So it is not the answer that is important, but rather that the asker stop posing the question.

Objectively and rationally, perhaps a cluster gene could be discovered. But what help would that be? It would be known that someone has a higher likelihood of getting headaches. A therapeutic approach will certainly not be further conceived within our lifetime. This doesn't mean that research should stop, because perhaps our children will benefit from it. And if it's our grandchildren, that is also a victory. But for now, we should stop asking questions that don't have an answer. Using that time for nice things definitely makes more sense. Since I started doing that I have felt noticeably better.

The way I recognise a senseless question may be a sensible question in itself. I think there are actually methods for detecting them. After all, a question only makes sense if the answer presents an advantage for me or benefits me in some other way. If no conceivable answer can do that, the most that it can do is satisfy my curiosity. Based on these considerations, as is often the case, it is at my own personal discretion to continue asking myself a senseless question. Nobody is forcing me to.

"You wrote that you aren't afraid anymore (or nearly) - are you no longer afraid of going to sleep at night? No longer afraid of the pain? No longer afraid that the medication won't work?"

No, I do not have these fears anymore. Although I can't exactly say why. Because it is terrifying to imagine that the medication will stop working, of course. But if I were to waste the time when the medication is working by imagining what it would be like if it didn't, well, that just doesn't seem sensible to me. It makes much more sense to enjoy that time.

Perhaps I would be scared to go to sleep if I didn't have an oxygen bottle and breathing mask right next to me. But they can be there. ALWAYS! For me, the tasteless, white, metal containers are the most beautiful decoration that I can imagine. I also like to look at the large oxygen tanks that every hospital has. They just calm me. So if you ever see someone standing dreamily in front of a hissing and icy steel tub, they are probably a cluster patient for whom this pressurised container is more beautiful than many others.

If there is anything I'm afraid of, it's that the medication I use will no longer be available. It would be a nightmare if nobody manufactured Imigran anymore. But until then I will enjoy living in a world with triptans.

"Have you sometimes felt that you are worth less than other (healthy) people?"

The short answer is a distinct yes-and-no. The long answer is, "Yes, but..."

I have felt so certain, but always formulated it a different way. I felt that I was not fulfilling the standards that had been set. Not in a relationship and not in professional life. I would not have been able to provide for a family and I could not work anymore. So I saw myself as pretty superfluous. Together with the childhood influences described in the chapter "More than Pain", any sense of self-worth was out of the question. I actually didn't want to live anymore. And, without medication, I probably wouldn't want to today either. During a severe pain attack I would have done something that I would not have been able to regret afterward. I am certain that I have my life of chemistry to thank. Long live the pharma industry! All changes in thought come from GlaxoSmithKline giving me the opportunity by discovering (and marketing) Sumatriptan. Along with Imigran (the brand name of Sumatriptan), the availability of Zomig (brand name of Zolmitriptan) and oxygen as a medical gas is fundamentally essential. Little will change in this regard for the rest of my life, most likely. The medications may change, as it is not impossible that more effective or compatible varieties will be produced. However, being able to completely abstain from them is out of the question for me.

That's enough about the past. What about today? Do I sometimes feel like I am worth less than healthy people? No! I have since become enraged because I think there are others who deserve a much worse disease than my own. And of course that is not ethically correct. But nor is the fact that I'm sick. It can also make me angry that I can't do everything I want to. Even today, my brain regularly goes on the defence. I take my time when possible, and have learned to enjoy the moment. But that's why it doesn't make me happy when I wake up three times in one night from the pain and cling to my oxygen bottle while the healthy linger in their pleasant dreams. No, that does not make me happy.

But abstinence is also a virtue. Because I was forced to learn how to enjoy the moment, I have since come to see myself at an advantage. I see the chaotic world outside, chasing status symbols and striving to keep up appearances. People who think they have to do things without knowing why they're even doing them. They do it because that's how it is. Simply leaning back, listening to the rushing of the wind or the chirping of birds, is a great pleasure. There isn't a lot that tears me out from my reverie. I also cannot think of anything that I'm afraid of. The world will keep on spinning, no matter what happens. All I can do is my best. But chaos and stress are not a part of that (anymore). Keeping and radiating calm has become one of my specialties. No, I do not feel anymore that I am worth less than others.

"Who do you tell what you have, and who don't you tell?"

Essentially I tell everyone. I just don't tell people directly and hold it up to their eyes uninvited. "Hello, I'm Rafael and I have cluster headache," is not my traditional greeting. But it does feel liberating that I don't have to hide the disease. Because I am unwaveringly convinced that people who react dismissively should be removed from my social circle.

"How do you explain what you have? I find it hard to explain ... once the word 'headache' is thrown out there, people think, 'Oh yeah, I've had headaches before, too.'"

Yes, unfortunately that's the way it is. And I don't see any simple way to change it. In the meantime I have also become uncertain as to whether a different name would be a solution. If a brief description is necessary, I describe it like a mixture between migraine and epilepsy. It comes and goes faster than a migraine, it is more severe, frequent, and can happen at any time.

"Do you ever feel that people around you do too little to address your disease?"

Oh yes, I had this feeling. And how! If I had never felt this way then I wouldn't have even begun writing this book.
But I don't feel that way anymore. Because the problem was not and is not with other people, but with myself.
An understanding environment is helpful. No doubt about it. A supportive partner as well. And a full bank account. But I cannot influence these aspects at this moment in my sickness on my own anymore. I would like to, but I cannot. This does not work if the patient has a broken leg, or cancer, or cluster headache.
But in order for somebody to address me, they must first know how I'm doing and what I'm having problems with.
To name one example: with this book I have shared my story with many more people in just a few weeks than in the ten years beforehand. One point that my social circle

responded to very quickly and practically was the despised question about how I'm doing. "How's it going?" So instead, for example, people ask about where I am on the curve. Is it going up or down? I never phrased it that way, but a friend of mine from yoga had the idea. And it's much easier for me to respond to.

"Have any of your friends seen you during an attack?"

During an attack I shy away from the public like pill bugs from light. It's always been like that, it is like that, and I don't expect it to change. I'm not doing at all well during an attack and don't want any company.
Only a few people have actually seen me in that situation. And in the time before the diagnosis I was completely withdrawn.
But how many are a few?
I have never kept a tally, so I can only estimate that in the years before my diagnosis, five to ten people saw me in the middle of an attack. The number is much higher post-diagnosis. However, the circumstances are very different. They only see me five minutes after I have taken Imigran. I will continue to hide from the public. Yet I have stopped hiding it from friends and even partners. Still I prefer not to be in a group. There is always a side room or a balcony where I can quickly slip away. But "hiding" is not exactly the right term. In that moment I don't feel good, not good at all, and don't want to explain things to anyone. Especially not when I'm sticking a needle into my arm. It's a tactical retreat. When using Imigran inject I can answer questions in five to ten minutes. If I'm sitting in a side room next to my oxygen bottle, then in half an hour.

"I can no longer meet the expectations that people have of me."

Granted it's not exactly a question, but a shocking revelation. It's closely related to the question about feeling like you're worth less. The topic warrants a brief philosophical discourse.

Being ill with cluster headache is not compatible with today's largely consumer- and performance-based society. There's no doubt about that, but it also applies to other diseases. Everything that lowers your productivity makes you a less attractive resource. This is a professional problem, no question, that cannot be alleviated. None of us have the power to change the economic system.

When it comes to cluster headache it's more intricate and difficult to convey than with other diseases or disabilities. For example, someone who loses their arm in an accident is entirely unable to avoid the consequences. They are also very visible to everybody around them. Such a situation, as dreadful as it may be, is extremely easy to communicate. But the cluster headache patient is on the other end of the spectrum. They don't know their specific limitations throughout the day. A specific and constant disability, like the aforementioned lost arm or blindness, is more predictable both for yourself as well as your surroundings. And if you don't meet your own expectations, or can't even formulate them, how can other people be expected to? They cannot even know the shape of your performance throughout the day, because you certainly cannot say it yourself for the next hour.

It is thus downright inevitable that expectations will not be met. At least with a proper medication regimen, you can come closer to meeting these expectations and greatly reduce outside pressure by being open. These are admittedly the wrong prerequisites for a career with a 60-day workweek. And the cycle ends. Illness is not compatible with our world - let alone cluster headache.

But where does this world come from, this world in which the sick don't fit? Have we people not done this ourselves? We have! We are devouring our fossil fuels, which accumulated over millennia, in an extremely short geological period. We are mercilessly robbing the planet of its natural resources and are uninhibitedly tearing scars into the environment. The trend to be as wasteful with these resources as possible does not seem like foresight to me. An unnecessarily large car in front of an unnecessarily large house impresses a lot of people. No matter where you look, the waste of resources is a status symbol. I leave why that is, and the considerations as to why we humans need status symbols, to philosophers like Richard David Precht. For me personally, it's enough to know that that's just the way it is. I cannot change other people, but I can change myself.

I think it's more difficult when it comes to expectations in your private life. Having to let a spontaneous visit to the movies fall through or ending a nice dinner halfway through also requires sacrifice and certainly a lot of patience from the other party. A great deal of patience. The people who contribute this patience cannot be bought, sadly. One can only hope that they will be there when needed.

And at least that same patients that other people provide must be given to oneself as well. That is the true difficulty in my eyes. I will even venture to claim that many expectations that one can no longer meet do not come from others, but from oneself.

I can no longer do everything the way I would sometimes like to. Some not so quickly, and some not at the time I want. So ideas are always building up in my head, which is in turn not free enough to implement them. Or the next attack will come in between them. As a result, I accomplish less. The bottom line is that productivity is lost. It's bitter, no question. Otherwise I never would have felt the need to write this book.

Yet it now seems to me that my lack of productivity has given me a great deal of awareness. So let's do things that we will remember fondly when we are old. Or, to quote Jack Kerouac, "In the end, you won't remember the time you spent working in the office or mowing your lawn. Go and climb that goddamn mountain."

Do what you can and do what you want. Don't pay too much attention to what other people want from you. Self-determination is not just a nice word.

Appendix

A conclusion, the "Yellow Pages" for headache patients, acknowledgments, an epilogue, and it had recommendations for other fascinating, helpful, and insightful books in the german edition. Unfortunately these books are only available in german language. Therefore I decided not to present them here.

Every person has the chance to improve at least part of the world - namely themselves.
Paul Anton de Lagarde

Conclusion in Key Points

What has been really helpful to me?

- A high dose, at least 720 mg, of Verapamil per day. Greatly reduces the number of pain attacks, and comes with just as distinctive side-effects.
- Oxygen for respiration via a mask in order to alleviate the intensity of attacks and shorten their duration. Special non-rebreather mask with an on demand valve HIGHLY recommended.
- Zomig nasal has given me pain-free periods of twelve hours in the worst phases. But this time should be used for doing more of whatever makes you happy.
- Imigran inject. The triptan injection for truncating a pain attack with the chemical enzyme in an emergency.
- Willingness to be unable to work. If you can't do it, you can't do it, and it's really important to take a break. Slaving away until you collapse is counterproductive.
- Good logistics for prescriptions, medications, and oxygen.
- Yoga helps me find peace and happiness within myself.
- My bicycle was always my best therapist and it will continue to be so. While cycling I can contemplate and reflect in peace, or maybe enjoy nature. On my bike I strengthen my ability to overcome the next episode. And on my bike I have learned how to work with limits, where they can be pushed and where they must be taken seriously.
- A person I did not want to sit across from with my shoulders stooped was always the necessary jump-start to return to life after a lengthy pain episode. I was sitting across from a doctor who was also an

impressive woman, and through the haze of Imigran clouding my eyes I saw how she took my hand and held it like she would that of a beggar. I did not want to take on that role.
- The medication is important and necessary, but without an actively changed attitude they only alleviate the symptoms. During my symptom-free periods I prepare for the next episode. Anything else would be superficial to me. But I also try to make as many positive memories as possible. These, not constant complaining, really help me come out of the other side of dark times.

Contacts / Internet Addresses

There are doctor and patient associations in many countries, and the International Headache Society towers above them all. It can be a very good contact if the local doctor proves unable to help. National patient societies and self-help groups often keep lists of doctors to make it easier for other sufferers to find assistance. I strongly recommend looking here: http://www.ihs-headache.org/

Guidelines

Treatment of Cluster Headache: The American Headache Society Evidence-Based Guidelines.
https://www.ncbi.nlm.nih.gov/pubmed/27432623

ICHD / Guidelines
http://www.ihs-headache.org/ichd-guidelines

Doctors Organizations

American Headache Society
https://americanheadachesociety.org

Patient Organizations

OUCH - Organisation for the understanding of cluster headache
https://ouchuk.org

ClusterBusters
https://clusterbusters.org

Wikipedia

Most patients do no even know and doctors do not even know what the Wikipedia summarizes. Be clever. Use the advantage to be smarter.

Trigeminal autonomic cephalalgia
https://en.wikipedia.org/wiki/Trigeminal_autonomic_cephalalgia

Cluster headache
https://en.wikipedia.org/wiki/Cluster_headache

When it comes to information from internet forums, communities, and other means of unfiltered discussion, it should always be remembered that at all times, and everywhere, there is a certain "ambient noise". This is by no means headache-specific, but it happens here as well. Not every single opinion is representative and not every recommendation for action is really advisable. Some basic scepticism and a healthy serving of common sense don't hurt.

In a previous chapter I mentioned that clusterheads may tend to get loud, and this is certainly reflected in the forums. A rough tone is not necessarily meant to be taken personally, but is rather a consequence of raw nerves.

Acknowledgments

Lone fighters have it harder in life than other people. People with cluster headache have it even worse. So, I would like to use this section to express my gratitude to everyone who has supported me and given me new motivation.

Special thanks to: A, S, W, B, S & K

There were, and thankfully still are, many other people who did not turn their backs on me in all these years. They include doctors and therapists, friends, and even family members.

Epilogue

I would like to leave this epilogue here for Saskia. She was my next-door neighbour during my rehabilitation in Bad Wildungen, and she wrote this poem for me.
I hope you're doing well.

Moulded by a life of pain –
Searching for the meaning to be learned,
The person becomes so helpless
and no longer knows where to turn.

The pain becomes ever greater, the person so small
Slow realisation:
NOTHING WILL BE THE SAME AT ALL!!!
The future casts 1000 shadows –

All existence merely breaks the light,
No hope left – no land in sight.
Time heals no wounds,
It is in union with death
And with every hour, late or soon,
It simply steals more breath.

But not all is only black,
There is also a lot of white.
When, in life, the price is right.

Those who have not experienced pain have not gained,
The sun only comes out after the rain.
And those who were never low were never higher.
Those who have not fought burn like fire.

Never give in –
Turn your head toward persistence,
The key is LIVING,
Not mere existence.

About the Author

Rafael Häusler

Born in 1970 in Recklinghausen, Germany. He graduated from school there and began studying mechanical engineering at the Ruhr-Universität Bochum. However, his chronic illness, cluster headache, nearly put his professional and personal life at a standstill.
The author now works as an IT specialist and media designer for a social services provider in Bochum and lives in Herne.

Find a supporting microsite for the english book at: http://ycswif.schmerzfrisstseele.de
The german edition is presented here: http://schmerzfrisstseele.de

If you understand german, you are welcome to visit my blog: http://seinplanet.de

Downloadable headache journal templates: www.schmerzfrisstseele.de/kopfschmerztagebuch/

You can find me on Facebook and Twitter and I can still be reached via old style e-mail: rafael@seinplanet.de

**Everything is going to be fine in the end.
If it's not fine it's not the end.**
Oscar Wilde

Supplementary Texts

The following texts were not released within the german book. They are taken from the additional blog, I use to write to keep up with new thoughts and therapies.
It is so far written - and will be continued - in german language, cause this is my mother tongue.
If you understand german, you are welcome to join the blog on http://seinplanet.de/category/kopfschmerz/.

"Never regret a day in your life:
good days give happiness,
bad days give experience,
worst days give lessons,
and best days give memories."

What Happened?

... and what will happen next?

About 15 years ago a headache the likes of which I had never encountered entered my life. Intense and merciless, it would not be alleviated with a few pills. It derailed my life and it would take a good five years before I received a diagnosis and this pain that changed everything was given a name: cluster headache.
Stupid name - stupid disease.
But I cannot think or wipe it away, so I had to deal with it.
Because I have never really felt like I'm in good hands despite the diagnosis and a bag full of medications, and especially because I never really felt understood, the idea to write a book hatched in my head in 2009.
When nobody listens to me, I scream at everybody. As an average citizen, I can do that best through a book.
So much for theory.
Thankfully it happened differently. *Schmerz frisst Seele* became more than screaming at everybody.
Because with this idea, everything actually got better. Not with the press of a button, not by a long shot. But an idea was also a goal. And things happened on the way to this goal that definitely deserve to be called "positive turns of events." I'm not cured. That was never to be expected anyway. Yet, strangely, many people dream of it. I continue to have headaches but I handle them entirely differently now.
Now there are things that happen only once you have written a book. They just continue to develop. And there are things that you only notice afterward.
One of these things is that writing was actually quite good for me. "Writing is reading yourself," says Max Frisch, and it's not included in the book for nothing. Writing means sorting through your own thoughts and reflecting on them. It helps deal with difficult situations.

Cluster headache is one such difficult situation.

I don't know if it's helpful for everyone. It is for me. That's why I decided to continue writing. To continue the book as a blog.

Here I would like to cultivate other lengthier thoughts that Facebook and other social media would not be the ideal space for. I'm very excited to see if the (hopefully) cultivated thoughts also lead to fruitful dialogues.

Thanks

They say that an artist is nothing without applause.

Now I'm not really an artist. I also wouldn't call myself a writer. Rather an author. And with another book I would have met the relevance criteria for my own Wikipedia article.

I'm not doing this all for the fame and to be celebrated. That was never my motivation and it certainly never will be.

I wrote the book for myself, essentially. And I was alone with the assorted thoughts of the first person to benefit from it. It was more a hope than a goal for me to pass it on to others. There's still a way to go to the Spiegel bestseller list, but a large number of people have read the book in the meantime and my wildest dreams have even been more than fulfilled.

When other sufferers tell me that they see themselves in what I write and my words can give them new perspectives, then I achieved what I wanted to do. It makes me really happy when people tell me that my words gave them courage.

Thank you!

The book wouldn't make much sense if nobody could do anything with it.

It makes me especially happy when people who don't have headaches at all are still able to find a way to benefit from the book.
They just liked it.
Even if "like" is kind of a weird word to use when it comes to the nature and content of it.

Thank you for that as well.

Another thank-you goes out to the people without whom none of this would have been possible, and without whom it wouldn't have happened if I were not so lucky that, in the end, it did. Because I had long since stopped believing in something that can be called a happy ending.
Thanks to Saskia, who was the first who had to hear my thoughts: "I'm writing a book. What else should I do? No one's listening to me. So I'm writing a book."
Thanks to the doctors and therapists who, in the meantime, decided to start listening to me.
Thanks to the publisher Pomaska-Brand Verlag, who believed in the project and with whom I feel very well looked-after and in good hands to this day.
Thanks to the always friendly women at my pharmacy who never left me in the lurch.
As I sat depressed in the wellness park of Bad Wildungen in 2009, I could never have imagined it would turn out like this. Still, in that sour-faced moment I did something important for which I should actually thank myself. I set a goal.

Education in Hamburg

This past weekend I took part in the officially titled 2nd Nationwide Cluster Self-Help Group Meeting at the Hamburg University Clinic Eppendorf, which Dr. Arne May had invited to.

The speakers Stefan Evers, Arne May, Jan Hoffmann, Charly Gaul, and Tim Jürgens are largely well-known names in the headache world. And I have seen most of them at various events in the past.
The schedule itself held no surprises, but why would there be. This was the full programme:

- Differential diagnosis: What is a cluster, what are the differential diagnoses?
- Where does cluster come from, and why is it here?
- Guideline-conform cluster treatment. Often propagated, not so often carried out.
- What to pay attention to: Comorbidities and courses of life.
- What to do if guideline-conform treatment doesn't work?
- When should I receive outpatient/inpatient treatment?
- News about cluster operations: Effective and safe? Which ones, when, and when not?
- Round-table discussion: Meet the expert

When I talk about "no surprises", I definitely don't mean that in a disparaging way. Anyone who shows up to this event "unprepared" would definitely go back home with smoking coming out of their ears and an abundantly full short-term memory. But because the mills of headache research grind slowly, there were no major changes to similar presentations from last year. Just like those had no dramatic changes from the year before. That's the nature of the matter. Of course, I'm happy that the mills are working, even though a litany of questions has gone unanswered for years now. Why do paroxysmal hemicrania and hemicrania continua respond to indomethacin while cluster and SUNCT do not?

In summary you could say that we still don't know the details of where cluster comes from, let alone why it exists. But there is also no specific answer as to why some medications help. However, the ideas for potential answers are becoming more concrete. Arne May predicted that we will have an idea for curing cluster headache by 2025.
All of the presentations were filmed and should be available online soon.
I especially liked the two presentations that dealt with the issue of the guidelines. It remains a mystery why these guidelines, which have been available to absolutely anyone for many years, are shockingly rarely adhered to.
This has resulted in the headache outpatient clinic of UKE's experience that it has to be checked in detail whether patients who are (reportedly) beyond treatment were treated in strict accordance with the guidelines, which is often enough not the case. Unfortunately this is congruent with our own experiences in self-help.

Among all these presentations were three pieces of information that stuck with me the most.

Ex-smokers have fewer attacks
This was a slide that stated that clusterheads who gave up smoking actually had, on average, fewer attacks in following episodes than before. Even though it's known that nicotine per se played a partial role in the occurrence of cluster in the House of May, these numbers are a head-scratcher.
Capsaicin

There were actual experiments with capsaicin ointment. It's reported that smearing it in the nose helps in some cases. If I'd heard that on the street, I would have filed it in the cabinet of curiosities next to willow bark covered in fox urine. It remains unanswered whether that which makes pepper and chilies spicy actually has an effect, or whether it's yet another manifestation of the all-powerful placebo.

Depression
After comparing the effects of chronic cluster, episodic, and migraine, the depression among episodics outside of their phase, i.e. in remission, was the greatest!
And so, bizarrely, I'm happy that I have always said that we are traumatised. Even though I would have preferred to be proven wrong.

The very new options via invasive (Pulsante from SPG) and non-invasive (gammaCore from electroCore) are simply too new for a definitive assessment.

Even newer, and thus not assessable at all, are the CGRP antagonists. If these function as hoped, then they will be the next big revolution in headache treatment after triptans. The first studies with cluster headache patients are underway. Now all we need is a little patience.

But the fact that there is an outlook of new procedures and treatments is fascinating, and provides hope that the situation will definitely get better and not worse over time. For the foreseeable future, however, it seems that the cluster headache patient will be a very active patient. One who educates themselves about their disease, who intensively observes themselves. One who tries the available medications to find the best treatment for them personally. No doctor can guarantee which triptan will be the most effective and tolerable. Nobody can tell you in advance whether Verapamil or Topiramate is the better painkiller for you. Only your own body can. Unfortunately it's complicated and costly, but there's no sensible way around it.

In the end, the meeting's name remains sort of a minor mystery. Outside of CSG I'm not aware of any "free" self-help groups. That doesn't mean that they don't exist, but it would surprise me a little. They would be very inconspicuous. Nobody from self-help was involved in the organisation or execution. Self-help's work was deemed necessary and important, but two sentences were all that could be spared on the matter.
So the event's name is more or less arbitrary, and it may be an autistic trait of mine to preoccupy myself with such a matter of semantics. I also noticed a shocking number of minor inaccuracies in the presentation slides. "Verampamil" and "atatcks" were the highlights of the weekend. Even worse (for me) are missing or double spaces. Of course, we are all only human, and I will certainly have hidden some errors in this blog post myself. If you find any, you can let me know. I'm happy to go back and correct them.

Bochum Cluster Headache Day 2015

The next education session in Bochum

The cluster headache scene is a blow-by-blow world. After the event last weekend in Hamburg, there was another small educational seminar in Bochum this week.
The reason was actually a postponed presentation of the large Patient Day in February that was caught back up and supplemented with current information on SPG stimulation.
Luckily for me, the commute was much shorter this time since Bergmannsheil in Bochum is only 3 kilometres from my work.

The schedule entailed:

Seminar and workshop for patients and loved ones.

Universitätsklinikum Bergmannsheil Bochum, Saturday, 09 May 2015, 9:00-11:30

- Fundamental research on the formation of cluster headache: Where do we stand today? (Prof. T. Schmidt-Wilcke, Bochum)
- Medication treatment insufficient – what comes next? (Dr. Ph. Stude, Bochum)
- What does SPG implantation mean for me personally? (Dr. T. A. Assaf, Hamburg)
- Exchanging experiences with patients

For five years now, when possible and feasible, I have been attending such patient days, symposiums, seminars, and workshops. About cluster headache, other types of headache, but also any other topic that relates to me or interests me. I'm very happy that I always have the opportunity. There is always a lot to learn. Both from the doctors' presentations as well as from conversing with other patients. The internet is a great thing, but personal communication simply has a few more dimensions. That's how it is and how it always will be. And I think that there is something new to discover in every new presentation on a familiar topic. There is always some aspect or new insight.

Thomas Alva Edison is supposed to have said, "If you think you've tried everything, you haven't!"

So today there were new things for me to learn as well. Namely, so-called harlequin syndrome. A rare form and capricious excess of trigemino-autonomous symptoms often associated with cluster headache. The hanging eyelids, the runny nose, the watery eyes. All of that happens on only one side. It's the same with harlequin syndrome. Upon physical strain or sweating, this happens on only one side of the face. One half becomes red, the other remains pale. A strange twist of nature.

Fundamental research is sadly still faced with a critical question: is activity in the hypothalamus an action or a reaction? Does it ultimately trigger pain in the brain, or is it a reaction to the pain? Imaging procedures have unanimously shown for years that something is happening in the brain during a cluster attack. However, it's not the only place in the brain where something is happening at that time. We do not yet have the right medical device that could show with sufficient temporal resolution where exactly that storm in the brain is happening.

Verification of cluster headache via an organic abnormality would be new and fascinating. A chance in the body that medical technology can document. There is nothing like that. No X-ray, no MRI, and no EEG can show in any way that someone is affected by cluster headache. One new idea in this regard is the thickness of the nerve fibre in the cornea of the eye on the affected side. According to initial observations, it is significantly smaller on the affected side than on the other. These nerve fibres can easily and quickly be imaged with a cornea microscope.

This idea is still in its infancy, and anyone who wants to take part can get in touch at kopfschmerz@bergmannsheil.de.

I cannot assess whether this idea will become a certainty. But I am convinced that it would be a great diagnostic tool. Since the procedure is really harmless, I call on everyone to participate.

Along with diagnosis, it's hoped that in the future nerve fibre thickness can be used to deduce the chances of success of different types of treatment. Because there are a great number of treatment approaches now, it would be more than helpful to be able to determine in advance which one has the best chances of success for the respective patient. That would be personalised medicine in cluster headache treatment.

One of these potential treatments of SPG stimulation of the sphenopalatine ganglion. Bergmannsheil in Bochum is working very closely with the UKE in Hamburg on this topic.
Measured by the number of removed appendixes and gallbladders, the number of patients operated on so far is rather small - we're talking about 200 in Europe. It is thus all the more exciting to see how the system - especially the implantation of the stimulator itself - continues to be developed. Navigational surgical technology is used with which the surgeon can use a calibrated tool to implant the stimulator in the depths of the fossa pterygopalatina at 2mm on the right spot via triangulation.

What is this SPG stimulation anyway, and how does it work?

The idea is that the sphenopalatine ganglion (SPG) is largely involved in cluster headache. If I exert electrical stimulation in this exact spot, I can disrupt the chain of signals and end the pain. Now, unfortunately the SPG is rather awkward and not that easy to access. So an incision is made in the upper gums, and a shoehorn-shaped tool is used to push the stimulator over the upper jaw and up behind the eye. If the patient's anatomy poses no challenges, it's over in less than an hour.
This stimulator is a passive component that is provided the necessary energy via induction.

This procedure requires so-called treatment-refractory cluster headache. As for what treatment-refractory actually means, that's still being discussed.

Because SPG stimulation is an invasive procedure and is thus still prone to possible complications, everybody is looking with great interest and criticism on past experiences. A pool of 83 patients would have been ideal (83 the number of all patients operated on in Germany so far, 53 in Hamburg alone).
Yet 44 patients were not available.
A patient cannot be forced, but for so many patients to refuse to return to such a small procedure that was recently classified as an experimental treatment, thereby making following patients' decision more difficult and ultimately hindering the development of the procedure, is shocking and sad. Shame on you!
Back to the available figures.
Of 83 patients, 44 went missing. Of the 39 remaining, 2/3 were better, 1/3 was not, sadly.
These are fresh results, and the complete study will be published soon.
We're talking about alleviation or improvement. Not pressing a button so that everything will be sunshine, like those adverts for sore throat and headache pills.
The stimulation can even result in short-term deterioration, as reported by a patient who had a successful operation. He talked about having to bite through it, and that it was worth it in the end.

That reminded me of the attack management mentioned by Charly Gaul last week. Whether it's the administration of oxygen or SPG stimulation. Cluster headache is not a simple disease by any means, and all sorts of mistakes can be made while working with it (unfortunately). And the great number of treatment approaches, some of which are still very young, also doesn't make it easier to pick the "right" procedure. But I prefer to have this problem than to have no options for treatment at all. And if we look back just 30 or 40 years, that's where we were. Without any type of meaningful option.

Even though nobody knows where we will be in 30 or 40 years, thinking about it in context certainly gives me hope. As Prof. Arne May predicted in Hamburg last week, "By 2025 we will have an idea as to how to cure cluster headache."

From the Headache News 01/2015

The Headache News is issued by Prof. Diener of the Neurological University Clinic Essen at the order of the German Migraine and Headache Society, and is available for download at: http://www.kopfschmerz-news.de/

I am always hearing from patient groups that there is so little research. Naturally, current headache research isn't covered on the daily news. But that doesn't mean that there's no research, no experiments, and sometimes simple testing. The Headache News, or Kopfschmerz-News, is a sort of German-language summary of what is going on in the international headache scene.
If that's not for you, you can read *Cephalalgia*. It's a monthly medical journal exclusively about headaches: http://cep.sagepub.com/

Of course, both publications mainly deal with migraine, which is much more frequent than cluster headache. Also these publications are not laid out as patient information, so you will have to work with the somewhat cumbersome medical jargon.

From HAN 1/2015

Here, too, things are tried out that lie somewhere between remarkable, bold, or desperate. One of them is "intranasal cooling". There's even a device for this strange combination of words. If you're interested, take a look at "RhinoChill". Because this cooling aid is pretty popular for

migraine at least, a professional cooling device should still be used only under controlled conditions.
It's a little harder for me to figure out why migraine patients insert a special balloon system into their nose that oscillates as it pumps up at a frequency of 68Hz. Interestingly, both have a positive effect.

The following can be read about cluster headache in particular:

"The pathophysiology of strictly hemispherical, particularly severe headache attacks is not fully understood, despite the characteristic phenotype with autonomous accompanying symptoms. While early cerebral blood flow tests via SPECT provided relatively vague results, better solutions and newer methods point to the hypothalamus as a central element. The connection of rhythmically occurring headaches with the 'internal clock' seemed apparent. More recent studies question this connection, however, and prefer a network dysfunction of the trigeminovascular system or the entire cerebral pain matrix."

Now THAT'S a good start!
I'd translate it like this: We don't have any idea, but we assume it's something other than what we originally thought. It's half-clear who and what is involved, but not how. What is the trigger, what is just a reaction? What is actually the beginning of what we ultimately feel as pain.
For those of us who are affected, this pain and dealing with it are understandably the worst and the most important. The researchers seem to have strayed a little bit from this in their fundamental research. Frustratingly it's at the end of the chain. That's right and important, of course, because it's important to find and understand the trigger. Then the pain problem may get rid of itself. At least theoretically, since we sadly aren't there yet.

A few lines down, however, I come across statements like these that I cannot comprehend:

"Comment: This cross-sectional study very well illustrates the various states of cluster headache. The large number of patients in all three sub-groups allows for stable comparisons and broadens our knowledge. The pathophysiological understanding moves away from central generators toward dysfunctional networks."

I understand that this is right and necessary. But I recall a time when my emotional state did not allow for this insight. Because it unfortunately didn't help treat my symptoms. I was pissed - absolutely pissed!

Anyone who is going through that now, because their treatment is not kicking in and/or they are in a high period, may try being more lenient with the medicine men. They, too, are only people trying to do their job.

This brings me to the next article. I will boldly quote this header as well, since the publication's open to the public for download anyway.

"Neuropsychological tests of cluster headache patients exhibit depression more frequently and prove to be highly stressed by the disease. However, methodical defects limit the significance of this study greatly, so that no further conclusions can be drawn from the available results."

This is the moment when you employ all of the breathing techniques you've learned from yoga. What should I be mad about? Or disappointed at? It's a lucky rabbit's foot of evidence-based medicine. It just needs empirical evidence. That protects us from unstructured experimental treatments, but also can make life difficult sometimes. For example, the effectiveness of inhaling oxygen is essentially proven by a study, because it's long been clear that it helps. Not everyone, sadly, but many. The ongoing Prednisone study (PredCH) is trying the same for Prednisone. Its effectiveness is actually uncontested, but because there are no studies to prove it, the medication is still available for off-label use.

The attending physicians who work with headache in general and cluster headache in particular are, in my experience, quite well aware that many of us are at least not far from full-fledged depression. It's more about undermining this circumstance in order to hopefully be able to established some sort of psycho-neurological assistance at some point. But that is a task that would take generations. Because psycho-oncology - i.e. automatic psychological care for cancer patients - is anything but the general rule, it would be fatuous to assume that anything will change in the foreseeable future. Self-initiative is still the name of the game, along with self-responsibility.

On Creaking, Crunching, and Clicking

It's obvious, and hopefully already known, that I really appreciate cycling as a form of movement and the bike as a vehicle. But this isn't about some traffic revolution, even if a discussion about that is quite overdue.
It's also not about the positive effects of movement in general and endurance sports in particular. Rather about strange noises that a bike can make.
Because I like to extend the lifespans of old bikes with a little love, there are always things to repair and worn parts to replace. Different defects have different sounds. One stroke of bad luck, and a variety of noises will happen in quick succession or even at the same time. One noise may have been remedied immediately before a similar one manifests. Or one loud noise will drown out a quieter one.

Now it's time for a brand-new story, not from the sewing box but from the toolbox.

It started with a click. After several hours riding in the rain, a low-cost and rather poorly sealed pedal reached the end of its life and drew attention to itself with the characteristic clicking sound. Foreheard is forearmed. Replacing pedals is no big deal, but because noises like that are annoying I had to replace it at the nearest bike shop along the route.
The noise was gone. Almost.
There was still a clicking. Quieter and less frequent. But it was there, and it would become more noticeable in the following days. The inner bearing proved to be the culprit. Separated from the pedal by only the pedal arm, it is still able to make its own noises entirely independently. The fact that two components that are physically so close together begin to urge for their replacement within a span of weeks, while it can furrow brows and shrug shoulders, is ultimately nothing more than pure coincidence.

After the clicking was gone, a crunching joined the symphony. That was clearly the seat. Leather seats are prone to do that, right...?
I didn't have much time to reflect on the crunching, because a far more aggressive creaking entered into the mix. There are noises that are just annoying and actually announce the damage or wear of a component far too early. Depending on your mileage you can ride around with it for weeks, months, or even years. But there are also noises that are much more distinctive. Those that herald that the end is nigh. Those that will change your plans.
You do what the noises want you to do.
It's like with a baby. It gets loud, and depending on how loud it is the
baby gets fed, swaddled, or cuddled.
My new noise came from the freewheel of my back wheel, which I had to inspect only after initial doubt and a strong lack of desire to do so.
I have replaced the pedal and inner bearing, but if you want to replace the freewheel you may as well just save yourself the trouble and replace the wheel. Replace it with the one that was originally in the noisy bike, but which, because of continuous radial fractures, had to be switched out for the one with the creaking freewheel...are you following?
In any case old parts increase the tension, because you never know what the next repair will be.
The bike was now riding along so quietly that the crunching from the seat slowly became uncomfortable. But leather seats are known to do that...sometimes.
But sometimes something breaks off from the seat frame and so it makes a crunching sound. The broken part of my seat is called the clamping pin, and it indirectly caused the ever worsening noises under my behind.
Replacing the clamping pin with a clamping bolt finally gave me peace. For the time being. What do I get out of it? Nothing! Because it's raining.

But that gives me time to write down this thought process. Because what will this person tell us about the weird noises his bike makes?
Completely unrelated defects affected my bike more or less in immediate succession. And as irritating as it is, none of them have anything to do with one another and each defect has to be repaired in its own manner.
I'm twice as old as this bike, but I have to get by without any replacement parts at all, and am probably made up of a far more complex system.
So you should take a much closer look at the human body - ideally your own - than I did with my bike. Similar symptoms can have very different causes. Entirely unrelated things can happen one after another by pure coincidence, making it seem as though one were a consequence of the other. We humans tend to think in such chains of causation. It's not generally wrong, because there are definitely plenty of things that build on one another. But with aftereffects, I have to go back to the very beginning.
In any case: take a close look!
Because a lot rides on the patient, until further notice, because doctors often take less time to look you over than bicycle mechanics do with bikes.

On that note: Take care of yourself – Prends soin de toi – Береги себя – Dbaj o siebie – Zorg goed voor jezelf – مراقب باش خودت – Curam habe de te – Pas på dig selv – Kendine dikkat et – Ta vare på deg selv – Να προσέχεις – Pass auf dich auf, Jung

A Journey into the Fundamental Research of Migraine

The Brain Café of SFB874 at the Ruhr University Bochum is always holding interesting presentations for the average citizen, thereby providing insight into things that are

rarely found in the newspaper. The topic is always the brain, and mainly its little defects.
Because if something's not going right, we will find out why it's not going right.
That's called research. Or even fundamental research. Only a few people do it in the hopes of being able to help many.
It takes a long, sometimes very long, time. Not every route taken proves to be the right one. But even if the process of elimination can be frustrating, it's ultimately necessary.
Thomas Alva Edison invented critical appliances like the light bulb, and with that alone he definitely changed the world. But, with direct current voltage, he was banking on the wrong technology for the distribution of electricity.
Wisely, to this he said:
"I did not fail two thousand times. I merely found two thousand ways not to make a light bulb."
The fact that this lightbulb that once changed the world is virtually banned in Germany (at least) not 150 years later is another story entirely.
I think for the most part, "In order to have one good idea, you have to have many."
The Lucky Punch is a nice one, but it's a fairy tale.

Anika Hunfeld, faculty chair of animal physiology from the Biology and Biotechnology Faculty at Ruhr University Bochum, held a presentation on 21 October 2015 as part of the Brain Café's "Migraine - More than Just Headache" event to show us some of these ideas and how they are questioned and evaluated through research.
Unfortunately these ideas are not nearly as specific as a patient such as myself would like. Ultimately, it can all be summarised in one sentence.
Every possible stimulus can trigger a cascade of events for a person with the proper disposition, the climax of which is usually the pain phase of a migraine attack.
Sadly that is shockingly abstract and, at best, not very helpful. Potential stimuli and triggers were asked about,

and even here there are still misunderstandings and uncertainties to this day. The ravenous craving for chocolate is part of migraine and it's not a trigger. Because the pain will still come if you resist your sweet tooth. That has been known for years in principle, but certainly not everybody will consider that alone. Why this all happens and what the actual beginning it, nobody knows right now. This action-reaction and chicken-and-the-egg problem are hotly debated. Changes can be observed in a migraine brain, but are they triggers or consequences? Nobody knows anything for certain.

The knowledge of the actual pain is more specific. It is still widely assumed that an inflammatory reaction causes the blood vessels in the cerebral membrane to transmit pain signals. Why this process is even triggered to begin with, and why it subsides at some point, unfortunately remains a mystery as well. However, it is quite clear that a widening of the vessels is related to the transmission of pain signals, and it is also known that the messenger substance CGRP plays a role.

How is this tested? How does animal experimentation help? Do mice get migraine?

Apparently there actually are rats that have migraine. And by the way they act, they are just as sensitive to light as the average migraineur. If you administer the messenger substance CGRP to mice, they seem to become part-time migraineurs and also shy away from the light. The experiment in and of itself is often terribly mundane.

Yet the result of it is now the only currently available medication group - the triptans. As well as the CGRP antagonists that are currently still in the study phase. They would be the first prophylactic medication specifically designed for migraine. Personally I am hopeful for it, although I must admit that it's more a gut feeling than anything else. Rather a feeling instead of knowledge.

So, despite an interesting evening, there are ultimately more questions than answers. But based on my own range of experiences this is the case with almost all diseases. I

think the small minority are truly understood. And until the fundamental researchers have gotten to that point, it's important to take a close look and compare experiences. Because that is what makes up empirical medicine today. We compile the things that are proven to help the most people and use them as initial measures for new patients. It's called 1st-choice guideline-conform treatment. I also think that's the most sensible thing somebody can do.
And that is what we are actually able to do while the few continue to research in order to hopefully help many others in the end. Until then, I am consoled at least a little by the fact that insight from research up until this point does not contradict my own observations.

The Right Diagnosis?

When you're not well-provided for. You don't get any sufficient treatment, or worst of all no treatment that meets guidelines. If you don't get a sufficient amount of medication, or at the very least have to beg for it.
And that's a common sighting in self-help. Patients whose doctors prescribe them Sumatriptan in pill form, and oxygen via nasal prongs.
If you are being insufficiently cared for in those ways or a similar manner, the only possibility in my mind is that the attending physician only read the headlines of the guidelines. Or maybe it was an audiobook they fell asleep to a little too early?
The logical consequence, for me anyway, is that a physician who isn't familiar with the right treatment cannot really be expected to make the right diagnosis. Anyone who has had the misfortune of running into such a doctor should, for that very reason alone, get a head start on finding a second opinion for their diagnosis and then looking strategically for the right treatment. Yes, looking. That's all there is. Nobody can predict which of the boundless options will provide the best combination of

effectiveness and tolerability for the respective individual. And strategically means nothing other than starting with the most probable treatment. That is exactly why these are marked as the 1st, 2nd, and 3rd choice in the guidelines.

Finding a suitable doctor has since become much easier than it was just a few years ago. Online there are lists of patients and doctors themselves that pop up any time you type the words "cluster headache" and "list of doctors" into the browser.

Admittedly it would be nice if the state of care was so good that this self-initiative wasn't necessary. But until we reach that point, it's necessary.

The same also applies to migraine, as the number of insufficiently cared for and poorly informed patients is shockingly high. Here, too, simply applying the resources and methods that are available could prevent many hours of suffering.

Paths to Information

Or: Why Facebook is both a blessing and a curse.

We live in an age when one single tool makes it easier for us to obtain seemingly all information than ever before in human history.

The internet!

Unfortunately, we also seem to be living in an age when many aren't taking this opportunity. I don't know if they cannot use it, or don't want to. That one place where most people tend to gather online is, of course, also where most patients convene.

Facebook!

There are groups there for virtually every type of syndrome and disease. These are the online wing of traditional self-help, fed by individuals' initiative and sometimes also an "offshoot" of a clinic specialising in the topic. What they all have in common is that people in each of these groups voluntarily took the time to compile the most important information and most elementary tips. Another similarity they all share is that almost nobody makes the effort to intentionally read this provided information.
Quite often, this leads to one of two scenarios: a question is only answered with a link to the compiled and provided (basic) knowledge. It never seems to occur to anyone that they could have found the answer to their question in a more expeditious way.
Key phrase: Let me Google that for you.
Worst-case scenario, the asker will receive an unqualified answer at three in the morning, followed by an eventual, "That's what it said online."

In the second situation, it often happens that the recommended group search or access to a file uploaded to Facebook doesn't work with a smartphone. Key phrase: "I'm online with my mobile."
Dear information-seekers: if the whole thing is so important to you, then sit the hell down at a normal computer.

Social networks aside, compiled and secured information has been available for quite some time in the form of books. Over the years many books who specialise in headaches have published books on the subject. From Göbel, Gaul and Sacks to Diener or Gendolla, they all contain roughly the same information. Yet many patients who say things like, "I don't know what I should do," have never read a page of these books. Unfortunately, alongside proper, guideline-conform books by representatives of evidence-based medicine are a range of different books with a dubiousness recognisable from promises of healing. No primary headache can currently be cured any easier than someone can change their skin colour. Some people turn red in the sun, others tan.

On the one hand, more research is required, and on the other long established and tested treatments are not even used. That's a confusing, and in the long term very exhausting, contrast. Because to repeat the same thing over and over again like a mantra - at least for me - impairs the enthusiasm that I try to bring to social networks, particularly Facebook.
Now that's certainly not some problem unique to self-help and social networks, but here it's an unfavourable combination. We often have desperate searchers on one side and volunteer responders on the other.
Even when the internet was in its infancy, there was the net jargon "RTFM" - "read the f*cking manual". Support requests online nowadays can usually only be submitted after you're forced to look through the preliminary FAQs.

These measures were definitely not implemented out of boredom.

Presumably I cannot do much to change the fact that the world keeps turning and people are how they are. But I am allowed to express my disapproval and concern about it.

Heed the sources, try to find established knowledge first before asking about every triviality, and read past comments before you answer a question. And only answer it if you can make a well-founded, sensible contribution to the discussion.

My Booboo is Bigger than Yours

I am now in the 17th year of my cluster career, and I have spent the last 11 years more or less active in the self-help field.

There are many things that I have been at odds with. I have since become able to make many of them, but not all of them, tolerable.

But there are also general things that I can't get on with. Some of them I am less and less able to find any positivity in as the years go by.

One of them is that the headache patient likes to whine, grouse, and complain. The cluster patient is also happy to do so loudly and boorishly, whereas the migraine patient is much quieter and more subtle. This merely reflects the types of pain that have to be endured by each. The actual point that pushed me to write this article is the tendency to exaggerate.

Specifically I'm referring to one comment that I decided to keep months back. I intentionally forgot the source.

"I have permanent headache 24 hours a day (intensity always between 7-9)."

No, you don't.

Because then you would be writhing around on the floor all day long without end. You wouldn't even be able to write that message. It'd be as if somebody were to cut off your arms and legs in slices. But even that you would only feel up to the knuckles, because then you would faint. That right there can happen to us. You can experience a state of pain right on the threshold of a frenzy during an (untreated) attack for one, two, or even three hours. That's bad enough, and it doesn't have to be exaggerated. The whole thing's not a competition. It's not about having worse, longer pain. Somebody with one daytime attack can and should do something about it just as much as someone with five attacks during the day. Whether an episode lasts for one month or half a year, it doesn't change the fact that it should be treated. But the strategies to that end can look very different. That is exactly why it is so important to describe the duration, intensity, progression, and sensitivity of the pain as objectively and precisely as possible. It's not helpful to degenerate it all into a pissing contest.

The number of attacks also is not a sole indicator of something like a level of concern. In my headache journal I have long been calculating the number of attacks times the duration of attacks times the pain severity in order to calculate and record something like a level of pain. But, of course, it's merely a very rough, approximate value that should never be seriously compared to the pain of another patient. It's so that someone who's affected by it can present it.

Firstly:
Someone with four attacks per day is not automatically twice as worse off as someone with two. Naturally, it also comes down to the duration and intensity of the pain. Residual and background pain, or aura-like visions, also play a role. Maybe not. Four attacks per month can ruin a migraineur's entire life if they all last longer than 72 hours.

Obviously the number of attacks is the only thing that can easily be recorded and communicated. Maybe that's why some people like to limit themselves to it.

Secondly:
That's simply not what it's about. Or rather, not what it should be about.
We are not fans of "I'm worse off than you."
But somehow that seems to either be an inherent aspect of human nature, or of the headache patient in particular. Part of it is certainly rooted in the fact that their suffering is simply not taken seriously enough. Neither by their social surroundings nor by themselves.
This always results in the description of astronomical numbers of attacks under which the speaker is still able to trudge off to work.
Unfortunately, I do not currently see any conceivable way to change that.
Motivational reports along the lines of, "Look here, I have cluster headache and I still do great things," are nowhere to be seen. And I also understand that because it's hard to conceive something like that when your skull is droning. Add onto that the unpredictability so that you never really know how to go about doing it.
To that end it would be absolutely necessary. I primarily see bitterness and dissatisfaction among a great deal of people who suffer from headache and whose lives are really impaired and influenced by it.
For example, if I take a look at the pictures compiled for the ArteCluster project, virtually all I see are horror images that express pure pain, suffering, helplessness, and desperation. On the one hand I'm sympathetic because the very same things certainly lived inside me once, and to this day, on the morning after a night with multiple interruptions, I'm not thinking about birdsong and meadows of flowers. However, I have since become aware that these visualisations of pain and misery are indeed important and necessary, although I hope that creative

and motivating messages will also be given their time to shine in the future. Because the constant repetition of suffering is not entirely beneficial to the cause.

Get-well Wishes

In one chapter of the book I extensively covered the question about how you're doing. I determined that I do not at all like the done-to-death usage of the phrase, "How are you doing?"
There's something else that may not have become such a truism, but which I still have issues with.
And those are get-well wishes. Get well soon - that's the most common one anyway. And that, whether it's meant or not, is totally fine when it comes to colds and other sicknesses. It doesn't even matter if it's coming from the heart or not.
But do I say that to a cancer patient? A dialysis patient? Or somebody suffering from dementia?
It doesn't really seem reasonable to me.
Now it so happens that you can hardly learn more from any other source than from other patients. The more severe the disability that you have learned to live with, the more you can learn. Self-help representatives of a wide variety of diseases have this opportunity time and time again every year on Rare Disease Day. I always notice how immensely the constant pain must influence our lives; others have to live with far more destructive illnesses. They get fired or have a much shorter life expectancy. We "only" hurt and we are worried about still being able to do the job we do have. It feels purifying to talk to someone who doesn't talk about a level of disability, but rather a level of care.

What do you say to that?

Quite simply, you will hopefully wish them, with all sincerity,

All the best!

It's so simple that I wonder why I didn't think about it a long time ago. But I really didn't.

A Look to Our Neighbours – What is the Significance of Migraine

This is the title of an entry in Markus Dahlem's blog, which I highly recommend reading.

http://www.scilogs.de/hirnnetze/eine-frage-markus-dahlem/

Because I have long been preoccupied by this very same question, I want to express my views on the matter as well as possible.

Migraine has no significance - it is a side-effect.

Some people get red in the sun, others tan. The way that we react is handed down to us. Our genes, people say.
Nothing helps, it is how it is and it will remain the way it has been. People who get freckles had better wear a hat. From what I know about pigmentation and skin layers, nothing will change that. I have a certain disposition, it's mine and my body's, and I have to deal with it. A sunburn is a wonderfully simple thing that is pretty easy to find the cause of. It's also easy for the burned person to act accordingly. And because there are many grey areas between the two extremes, it's enough to put on sunscreen. Others wear a hat and long sleeves, or don't even venture out into the sunlight.

When it comes to migraine, the correlation between cause and effect is, unfortunately, neither easily nor directly attributable.

But migraine is not such a simple side-effect. It is virtually the price for an ability.

Even though it's contentiously debated, after about two decades of observation I am positive that there is such a thing as a migraine personality. Migraineurs tend to be diligent, conscientious, and devoted. We don't let things lay idle, and even complete other people's work. Migraineurs are perceptive. We see everything, even in our periphery. In crowds of people, or just at the supermarket, other people will walk past you because they are virtually going through the world with blinders an. A migraineur will be the first to take a look. Thanks to the lack of blinders, the migraine brain is barraged by stimuli from its surroundings, and once it's overwhelmed, up goes the white flag and it shuts down. Pain, withdrawal, break!

Why exactly is that an ability?

I understand it to be one that was once much more useful. However, since the invention of the blinking neon sign at the latest, those days are over. Mankind has set itself apart from all other fauna through specialisation. While one aimed with a spear, another had to make sure that nothing would come jumping out of the bushes. Groups needed such perceptive individuals so that everybody had a better chance of survival.

Yes, that is history now. But back to the modern day, not everybody is able to tolerate dairy. That is also a very old genetic inheritance.

I don't know if I'm right. We will probably never be able to know for sure. One would have to perform a scientific experiment on something that can no longer be experimented on. No idea how many Encino Men would have to be thawed out for that to work. But for me, this model adds up and at the very least it explains to me the migraine part of my head.

But what about cluster?

In my book I showed that my migraine seems to me like a jealous woman who only wants to look after herself. Unfortunately I don't know how to tran-scri-be the image for women, who make up the majority of sufferers. Sorry. But for me that's what it seems like. I don't think it's good that it's happening, but I can largely understand why it's happening. Cluster headache is distinctly arbitrary in nature. It is a wild beast that hurls everything standing in its way against the wall without prejudice. In fact, I don't have an idea or model for it. It's just there, and its unpredictability makes handling it a good deal more complicated.

I think that migraine is clearly the price I pay so that I can perform better than many other people. But when it comes to cluster headache, I have not yet had such an "epiphany". It's really just there, annoying me. But that doesn't mean that I can't learn how to deal with it.

Botox in the Pterygopalatine Ganglion

If you ask me, more treatment won't make it any easier.
But that is not the case, but rather just one study with 10 patients conducted in Norway from late 2013 to mid-2014. The results were just published in the current edition of *Cephalalgia*.
http://cep.sagepub.com/content/36/6/503.long

It's about a blockade of the pterygopalatine ganglion with an injection of botulinum toxin A, commonly known as Botox.

The approach is rather simple. The pterygopalatine ganglion is a ganglion located deep within the face behind the bridge of the nose and which is part of the autonomous nervous system and is supposed to play a critical role in the transmission of pain in cluster headache. Botulinum toxin A is a toxin that aims to paralyse this ganglion. More or less along the lines of the implant marketed as "Pulsante" for stimulating the pterygopalatine ganglion (http://www.ati-spg.com/europe/de/). Performing the procedure is no longer quite so trivial, because it's important to conduct CAT and MRI localisation to find the right spot. The words "general anaesthesia" are used in the article to describe the procedure.

The result gives just as much reason for hope as the others, and it's also equally as shocking. I think it's shocking at best, scandalous at worst, that the data of three patients out of 10 could not be evaluated because they did not report back with it. What's wrong with this person? Of the remaining seven, a few experienced significant improvement, some of them even over an excessively long period of time.

Unfortunately, and also thank God, cluster headache has a wide variety of possible treatments, although this poses a real challenge to doctors and patients alike. Right now nobody can predict which option will be the right/best/most effective for the respective patient. This could mean spending years searching for the optimum treatment.

How do you deal with depressed thoughts?

This is a question that is always asked, in some form or another. In traditional self-help groups and Facebook groups.

Can this question be given a generalised, succinct, and helpful answer? Or do numerous books have to be read, do you have to undergo treatment over a span of months? Or multiple treatments?

You don't have to, but you should - at least in my opinion. Such thoughts don't come to you in a quarter of an hour, so you absolutely can't jump right into them in five minutes. Quite the contrary, they can even entail hard work. And there is no panacea that can be used against it. But there is a sort of template.
Nearly all revelations about how to successfully deal with depressed thoughts say that you have to make a curve around them to make room for nice thoughts and memories.
So the question, "How do you deal with depressed thoughts?" can be answered with one simple word, if necessary:
Superposition!
That way I don't give the destructive spiral of thoughts any room in my brain.
However, everybody must figure out for themselves how successful this approach is for them.

For me, a lot of it happens on my bike. The feelings that Velouria describes in her wonderful blog post "The 12 Stages of Climbing Addiction" have always passed through my head during ascents, and they will continue to do so.
Side note: ascents are much nicer than headwind. Reaching a summit means achieving a goal. And there is a reward. The view and the opportunity to roll back down. Headwind is just wasted energy.
This happened quite distinctly during a recent trip to the Sauerland region. At the end of the SauerlandRadring cycling path there were too many hours of daylight left, and at one summit along the route was a transmitting tower. You could see it up close.

Said ... done.

Over paved side streets and wide forest roadways, there is crank turn after crank turn toward the top.

Admittedly, the transmitting tower itself is a steel framework just like any other.

But the view from the peak was definitely worth the effort.

It creates a memory that doesn't come for free, which makes it all the more vivid.

Migraine and Nitrates

When I was "eavesdropping" on the announcements during my evening podcasts, I sensed that there was some misery behind the reports once again.

The announcements can be found here:
http://www.deutschlandfunk.de/meldungen-liste-forschung-aktuell.1508.de.html?drn:date=2016-10-19&drn:news_id=668659

"People whose mouths have more bacteria that concert nitrate to nitrite experience more frequent, severe headaches like migraine."
So far, so good.
Researchers have compared the presence of such bacteria with subjects' answers to a questionnaire about often they suffer from migraine.
Nobody actually checked whether the subjects actually suffer from migraine and have been properly diagnosed accordingly. In practice, "migraine" is rather a very vague term as opposed to a firm definition.
When I have a herniated disk, it makes a difference whether it's around the lumbar or cervical vertebrae.
The report has been floating around the media landscape since yesterday, but nowhere can we find figures that would tell us how remarkable the correlation is.

Meanwhile, the rest of the theory is easy to imagine. A bacterium in the oral cavity - they're everywhere, but I believe that they aren't just there, but all throughout the digestive tract - converts nitrate from food into nitrite. In the circulation of blood, this nitrite can then be converted into vessel-expanding nitrogen monoxide. I have never heard of that before, and have to just believe it.
The idea behind it? A simple mouthwash as migraine medication.
Seriously: the bacteria are supposed to convert sufficient quantities in the mouth alone? Or do they also need the stomach and intestine? But then mouthwash probably wouldn't be enough.
Something about the story doesn't add up. As of right now, it's not a basis for research or verified knowledge, but rather a finding by happenstance.
That's not bad, it's how penicillin was invented.
But it can certainly be researched further. Headlines like "Migraines Come from the Mouth" are beyond misplaced.
It's a shame that even the radio has descended to the level of click-bait.
Phrases like "potential trigger factor" are more accurate.

Fear, Part 1

I have been pregnant with this blog post for a few weeks now, but despite the time I've given it, it doesn't seem to want to come out. Before I lose my thoughts in endless spirals, I want to write down their interim state here. It will also help me get them out of my head.
That's another big benefit of writing something down.
What's been written has been written, and so your everyday thoughts don't have to revolve around it constantly.
The topic in question was, or rather is: fear.
I was occasioned to write it after two conversations with migraine patients, both of whom suffered from severe anxieties and probably still do. Both had no experiences with triptans for curtailing their migraine attacks at the

time. However, before ever swallowing a single pill, they both had an uncertain fear of medication-induced headache, or even medication dependency.

An entirely real, existing fear for a completely irrational reason. It's hard for me to put myself in those shoes.

Because I had not had fears like that. Not to any extent. I was ecstatic that there was medication that could help me. I would have taken anything that promised relief, without prejudice. This is where the migraineur differs from the clusterhead. And I'm not surprised in the slightest. A person conforms to the pain that inevitably shapes them, to a degree. As a hybridhead I know both sides, but I can hardly comprehend these fears of a migraineur.

While I tried, there were some reports about Daith piercing brewing on the web. I saw them, but I have better ways to spend my time. I'm happy to say that my friend Markus A. Dahlem, on the other hand, has taken the time.

Hope and hustling seem to have a magical relationship with one another.

However, I like evidence-based medicine. It makes mistakes, owns up to them, and improves itself accordingly. Many alternative procedures don't do that. That alone is a reason to not take it seriously. The health insurance company/pharma industry system so often demonised in some circles isn't that bad to me. They are in competition and want to earn money while giving out as little as possible to the other. There's something self-cleansing about it.

But I'm getting excited. People in other places believe in the effectiveness of ground rhinoceros horn. Not everyone is able to use their brain to their benefit.

But I digress. A lot.

So back to fear.

What kind of fear is this anyway?

Are we talking about naked fear for one's own survival? Or rather from the worry about not being able to meet some sort of standards?

I cannot really answer this for other people. But for myself, I know that I could probably develop anxieties if I were to let these standards still apply to me. I have actually pushed a lot of things that could have caused anxiety away from me and out of my life. Not everybody will be able to, or want to, act so radically. I also cannot expect everybody to.

What I can truly recommend in any case is rationally addressing the specific fears. Does it have a real basis in the situation, or am I just talking about the devil until he shows up? In the second instance it will hopefully help to envision it more and more until you cannot talk about him anymore. It may be good that this does not work in a slide, but with one's own knowledge. It may be necessary to practise this.

And what fears do I have now? Are there really any left?

If I'm afraid of anything, it's the lack of the medication that I use. It's hypothetical.

If all manufacturers of Suma- and Zolmitriptan ceased production, I would be scared shitless. There have been continuous bottlenecks in the recent past, but I personally was fortunate enough in that the delivery issues occurred during my remission phases.

Knock on wood!

Before I have any more thoughts about fear, for the moment I would like to close with the old wisdom that fear is a poor teacher.

Fear, Part 2

May contain traces of inspiration from @manomama.

We were not quite through with the topic of fear.
After all, there is a frightening amount of things you can be scared of.

But what is at the core of this fear? Think about it philosophically. Or from a kitchen philosophy perspective, because I didn't study that. Or evolutionarily. As well as the kitchen version of that.
Being afraid of the right things can save your life. Fear of sabre-toothed tigers, for example.
Though it so happens that they are extinct and we are not.
Only rarely do we talk about this type of fear in many parts of the world. In some, sadly, we still do. But that's another topic.
What could I have to be afraid of?
Fear of scary clowns? Ah, nobody can even remember those days anymore.
Fear that the Americans will actually be able to elect Donald T. to the White House? Well, they've since done that.
Yes, fear of that is justified. What I wonder is if I should be afraid of the person themselves, or of the fact that somebody who exhibits such disqualifying behaviour can put himself in public office and still have half the population behind him.
Fear that there is a shocking number of people who still follow him despite everything, and who continued to follow similar figures throughout history?
That certainly gives me doubt.
Fear that there seems to always be people who do evil things to others and harm them in every conceivable manner. Whether it's unconscionably (only) to one's own (financial) benefit, whether men view single mothers as fuck bait [1], or rape them in - and after - war? In groups, premeditated, and organised.
It's nothing new. It happens every day on this planet. For centuries. At least.
North-Rhine Westphalia has around 100 women's shelters, and that is too few. They have to exist because there are men who can only articulate themselves to women through violence.

This is sad, horrible, and it makes me more than just doubtful. It makes me sick, and I am definitely afraid of that which lives at the very least in some people.
But those are other fears. Justified ones.
I'm also afraid that some authors whose yellowed works some of us read back in school did not exactly lead model lives. Virtually none of them abstained from experiencing with consciousness-expanding substances. One Heinrich von Kleist shot himself, and because he didn't want to do it alone, he "cast" a terminally ill patient to join him. A memorial now stands at the spot where he did it. A memorial, not a warning! And that is not the only one.
So does everybody need a memorial? Who the hell allowed that to happen?
Well, that makes me dizzy. But having to live among people who support that can make you a little scared. Having to reside alongside crowds who probably don't even know that Kleist once existed tears me apart. Jack London (The Sea Wolf) breathed his last breath after only 40 years, and his alcohol consumption was certainly not innocent. Only three years before his passing he published an autobiographical novel in which he discloses his addiction to the bottle. All in all, that helped...very little, roughly. Every exhibitor at Anuga still go to strange lengths to snag customers. There are a few beer carts in the brewing hall, and they are mobbed more than anything else.
More good reasons, but that's also not the right fear.

"Helicopter parents take their kids to school in the car because all of the cars have made it dangerous to walk to school." [2]
Aha.
Here I may be most afraid of the reactions of a narrow-minded pilot parent in the event somebody confronts them with the craziness of their actions. There are things that are so clear that nobody has to explain them...at least,

that's what I think sometimes. But in practice it looks a little different.
Fear? I don't really know. But I could scream. Loudly.
The path does not lead to the destination. Not for me, anyway. My fears appear to be different.
I do notice that these fears have something in common. I have no influence over them - the circumstances.
There are things that I simply have to just tolerate. Whether I like them or not. I can ignore them, forget them, suppress them, work on taking a different perspective on them or desperately struggle to see something positive in them. I can! But I cannot change them.
Now if I apply that to the sabre-toothed tiger, then I have really come face-to-face with fear. Eye to eye with a big cat that is not too keen to cuddle. If that's not enough, then the stereotypical, nauseous breath beating against you will be. This would be the moment when the body, pushed to the highest level of stress by hormones, shows surprising reactions.

So what is this fear actually, from a biological perspective? I think it can be seen as a state of stress and strain. What would such conditions do with people who suffer from migraine?
If you wish, you can lean back, breathe, reflect, and draw your own conclusions.

I kind of feel like redefining fear. I think that it is a step below what we often exaggerate it to be, and we end up not doing ourselves any favours.
Is that really fear, or just worry?
Am I afraid I won't be able to make an appointment over the weekend, or am I just worried I won't? And if I do want to call it fear, then what or whom am I even afraid of?
Is it ultimately not just the doubt that you will not be able to meet requirements? Whose requirements?

Based on my own observations and experience, the lion's share of "fears" is based on not being able to meet the needs of others and social norms. I am happy to admit that this is (very) aggravating and can keep you from your career for a long time, but fear is something different.
Once again, it ultimately comes down to a matter of evaluation. Because I don't have to meet others' expectations.

But because the migraineur is often hard-pressed to adopt this attitude, a second foundation of fear is laid over it. Even if the traditional daydream is not even generally negatively associated, the madhouse of migraineurs in the sky is not the traditional playground for the inevitable happy end. While playing the "what-if" game, we picture at least three corners in advance. This creates a wide variety of possibilities that one can prepare for.
First of all, this is not efficient whatsoever. The worse possibility will always win. "What if she doesn't call you?" That outmanoeuvres something else that's inefficient.
If you see yourself in that situation and want to make a change, then you will have to take action.

[1] https://twitter.com/manomama/status/790966746215841792
[2] https://twitter.com/land_pomeranze/status/791138441807458307

Diagnosis is Simple – Treatment is Not

A few days ago I heard a report on the radio about stuttering therapies that received an unexpected reaction. The expected result for nearly every disease these days (yes, disease. The doctor can diagnose stuttering with the ICD code F98.5, and it is thereby in the system as a defined syndrome. An official disease, as it were) is the knowledge that the proper treatment can only be provided after the proper diagnosis. And that the road there can be downright bumpy.

It seems different when it comes to stuttering. Indeed it's not visible, and diagnosis doesn't seem to be a big deal. But the issue is not addressed on the website of Bundesvereinigung Stottern & Selbsthilfe (BVSS - National Association for Stuttering & Self-Help).

With regard to stuttering, it's very clear what you have and very uncertain what you can do about it. There are guidelines and guidebooks that are not necessarily in agreement, and only very few of which have scientifically proven effectiveness. The National Society of Speech Therapists also doesn't know which procedures and treatments their members even use.

Working with stuttering relies mercilessly on the level of hearsay and Medieval approaches. It takes pure luck to find a woman speech therapist (there are apparently no men) who might bet on the right treatment.

On the other hand, stuttering has become a reference point for medical assessment work in the field of compensation rights and in accordance with the Disabled Persons Act (Part 2, Social Code IX) published by the Federal Ministry of Labour and Social Affairs. Put simply: stuttering is a recognised disability.

Migraine is in there too, but not cluster headache. Not yet, though I hold on to hope.

But there is actually great unanimity when it comes to headache treatment. Even internationally. For years we have been living with the fact that there are treatment guidelines and suggestions that are almost identical in content but that unfortunately not all doctors are aware of. This leaves doctors making false recommendations and writing unsuitable prescriptions out of sheer ignorance. Estimated realistically, this state of affairs will only improve over generations. Because even today there are practising physicians who were in medical school before triptans were invented. It would certainly go faster if every patient who has ever been falsely diagnosed or treated would confront their doctor about this with all

openness. But this - also a realistic guess - will probably never happen.
In the end I am aware that when the disease, the syndrome, or whatever, is entirely clear, it must not necessarily be entirely clear how to counteract it.

It comes down to a suggestion that every self-help organisation gives. This includes BVSS, who write on their sites:

Be an "expert in your own thing", because your college examiner or instructor generally has no, or very little, idea about stuttering. Explain it in an open discussion.

In closing, here is the link to the radio programme that triggered the idea for this post:
http://www.swr.de/swr2/programm/sendungen/campus/swr2-campus-streit-um-stottertherapie/-/id=658620/did=18282388/nid=658620/1ole5qk/index.html

Well-Intentioned – Accessibility

This is something that has not sat well with me for a while. A tweet from Laura Gehlhaar that references an interview with her in *Tagesspiegel* was today's trigger for writing a few words on the matter. Because even though it's a nice interview and I am completely understanding in principle, my other situation starting out does not really cause me to have a different opinion, but at least a different perspective.
And I would like to start with an anecdote.
Some time ago I was able to witness the dispute between two wheelchair-bound people at a national self-help meeting. The two were in disagreement about how accessibility can be realised at train stations. Wheelchair-bound Person 1 had no problems at Station XY, which Wheelchair-bound Person 2 saw entirely differently. These

two very contrary opinions, which I found surprising, bounced loudly off each other and I was not the only person in the room to unexpectedly gain some insight.

It's simple: don't get involved.

If wheelchair-bound people are in disagreement as to how their easy access to trains can be realised, then I would rather stay out of the issue.

To quote Dieter Nuhr: "If you don't have any idea, just keep your mouth shut."

But I know that this is only one form of accessibility. What if I'm missing limbs, or I'm only 1.2 metres tall? What if I'm blind, deaf, or mute? What if I have epilepsy or narcolepsy? Or migraine and/or cluster headache?

Different handicaps require vastly different types of compensation. And not all needs can be met with structural adjustments.

So are ramps by themselves a good start, or just consolation?

Unfortunately I also don't know what a comprehensive approach that satisfies as many people as possible would look like. A consistent degree of acceptance, tolerance, and understanding for every type of disability and all forms of "otherness" would be one desirable approach. Sadly the world's progress in terms of ethics and morals is not especially convincing at the moment.

It's time for a saying from grandma: "Treat others the way that you would like to be treated."

Wikipedia refers to it as the Golden Rule of practical ethics. Because it has been around for at least hundreds of years, or perhaps thousands in some similar form, my statement will hardly change. On the other hand, you all certainly had a grandma who used to say something along those lines as well.

Fear Part 3, on the Path to Inspiration & Motivation

… thought laterally while reading an interview in the winter 2017 issue of PainPathways magazine.
What do you do on a gloomy, rainy Advent - when nothing is hurting? Exactly! You read about what it's like when something is hurting you.
Yeah, sometimes that definitely seems rather oblique to me.

In any case, after first scanning through the online version of the winter 2017 issue of PainPathways magazine and reading the migraine article therein, I'm not as enthusiastic and excited. The publication is also a mixture of advertisements and matching articles. And, as is to be expected, it's not at all mainly about the head. But because the back is far different from the head, it doesn't all line up. When it comes to the cohesive management that one aims for in multimodal treatments, ultimately a lot of things are done the same way but one must be introduced to it differently in order to collect the patient and really take them with you. This does not come together smoothly for me in that instance, nor does it here.

But in the current issue there is an article specifically about the head. It's about American actress and migraine sufferer Bellamy Young. I don't know the woman, although she is the right age and she would definitely make my head spin if I saw her on the street. This is simply because I banished the glowing transmitter with my remote some time ago. Because not everybody has done that, maybe one of you will know her. She plays the spouse of the president of the United States in the series *Scandal*, Mellie Grant.
She has played her since 2012 and surprisingly has never had to take a day off from filming, as I learn in the interview.

"In her five seasons of playing Mellie Grant, Young has surprisingly never had a migraine stop production."

Now I wonder whether that means that she has never had a migraine while filming, or if she has covered it up well and continues filming while experiencing one.
While reading the next sentences I learn that she is afraid of that which does not happen at all. After the introduction, which talks about 18-hour days, I'm somewhat confused.
Migraine? Or not? Maybe just migraine lite? Always at times that happen to be convenient?
It's not always easy being the monk.
But in any case the fear seems to be there. The fear that I recently wrote about and no longer want to refer to as such. They are considerations, a worry, but not a fear!
Okay, the person affected sees it differently, but that is exactly why I will not reinforce him (or her) in that regard. I certainly get the sense that these worries tend to become more distinct for as long as nothing really destructive has actually happened.
Is it true that the worry that something could happen is greater than the worry that something will happen for the second time?
What do we now need so that "Information & Inspiration for Living with Pain" will function?
This identification thing, so to speak. Here is somebody with a similar fate who looks very pretty and is still quite successful. She takes a medication and half an hour later she is doing better, and it can all be turned around. To quote the interview:

"As long as she can take the pill before the tunnel vision begins, then the debilitating pain, nausea and sensitivity to light and sound won't manifest into a full-blown attack. She needs 20 to 30 minutes for the effects of the medication to take hold—then Bellamy Young can turn back into Mellie Grant and finish filming. When a migraine attack does occur on set, she praises the cast and crew of *Scandal* for being understanding and supportive of her need to take a short break before returning to finish work."

Now I'm stumbling over the recommendation to take the triptan before the auras manifest. To my knowledge, this is not advised here in my country. Then I remember migraineurs who, during an attack, no make-up artist in the world can turn into a photogenic face even with triptan. And in my own personal experience, a triptan has no such sweeping effect that I could keep acting "as though nothing had happened". It's actually a little hard to imagine, but should we not be all the more happy when somebody responds so well to the medication options open to them?

Yes, we should!

But it can seem difficult, right?

I believe at least part of the problem lies in why it seems so impossibly difficult to connect the issues surrounding migraine and cluster headache with "information & inspiration". The incomparability inherent in the invisibility.
It can be – but it just doesn't work for me, because ...
And you could always say that. Remove yourself from the situation and shed all responsibility. And that's also understandable and correct.
Mrs. Young takes her Treximet (a Sumatriptan/Naproxen compound that, to my knowledge, simply does not exist in Europe) and can carry on as Mrs. Grant. She can also definitely afford it and take a holiday. She has not lost her job and doesn't sit alone at home. Unfortunately, that does not work for me.
That, or a similar response, is how I imagine the reaction of those who actually do not experience such effective alleviation and improvement of their situation because of

a more intense manifestation, and have to deal very concretely with the greater impact on their lives.
I would much rather see someone who is doing worse than I am so that I can feel better. That is the perverse way in which our psyches work. I recently read an article along that vein somewhere and will be happy to find it if you want.

For the time being, I am certain of the following things:

The fear of getting wet is greater when you do not know how well you can swim.

The matter of motivation & inspiration when it comes to all things related to cluster headache diseases remains one of the great challenges in life.

In closing, here is a link to the interview with Bellamy Young: https://www.painpathways.org/bellamy-young/

Bochum Cluster Headache Patient Day 2017

I am indeed satisfied with my personal treatment options, but because of the deep infringements on my own life, I'm urged to keep up with the times like before things were this way. So last year I took part in a CGRP study and I enjoy attending presentations about headaches in general, and migraine and cluster headache in particular, and consider it a type of continued education. Much like yesterday's Bochum Cluster Headache Patient Day at the University Hospital Bergmannsheil.
When you're sitting across from your doctor for an appointment, how much time do you spend together? Only in rare cases will it be longer than 10 minutes. At such a patient conference, three doctors each speak consecutively for half an hour at a time. So they have a lot

more time - it's very mundane, actually - to impart information.
Each doctor has their own personal experiences and subsequent preferences and perspectives. As a patient, there is nothing more educational than listening to multiple doctors in succession. I've been doing it for many years, and of course the fundamental information is always the same or develops only slowly over time. But they develop at the same pace as experience and the actual research being conducted.
Conclusion: I'm all about patient conferences, symposiums, and so on!

Now for the specifics on the one in Bochum.

I missed the commencement speech because I had a problem hearing my alarm in the morning. But I entered a pleasantly full lecture hall just in time for the first technical presentation. Later I learned that I was counted as the 71st guest. For a rare disease, a sunny and warm early spring day, and another event in Münster, I think that's really good.
Dr. Storch from the Headache Centre in Jena spoke first about "Cluster Headache Medication". Along with the familiar and available options, there is an entire range of new possibilities on the horizon. This is partially because of new medication, but also newly discovered traits of long-established and familiar agents.
The new medications are the CGRP antagonists. Or rather CGRP-receptor antagonists. Or, to be more precise, calcitonin-gene-related-peptide-receptor antagonists. Numerous studies about them are currently being conducted, as multiple manufacturers want to work with the agent. And it is certainly the first time in history that studies are being conducted about cluster headache before medication is being put on the market. This is because the manufacturers want the agent to be effective against cluster headache and migraine.

The agents are still adhering to hardly memorable labels like LY2951742, AMG 33, TEV-48125, and ALD403. But we cannot really say when we'll be able to ask for them at the pharmacy. That's how studies are. They're finished when they're finished. Yet we can be certain that the "evil" pharma industry is very interested in it happening as soon as possible and will take the slalom through their safety and monitoring measures without any unnecessary delays. Ketamine, first synthesised in 1962, is part of the "been around for a while, but observations have shown that it can help" category. It's an anaesthetic that shows positive effects on cluster headache in sub-anaesthetic doses, as reported by initial studies.

Now let's get to two names that I had never heard a word about before: Ibudilast and Lasmiditan. The former is a medication actually used for MS, and the latter is a migraine medication still in the study phase.

And while I'm looking them up I think, "Why do they have names and the CGRPs don't?" But alas! That's not true. At the very least, Eli Lilly baptised his CGRP monoclonal antibody LY2951742 as Galcanezumab.
Take a look: https://www.lilly.com/pipeline/10.html

On to two topics that are always rather difficult to discuss objectively.
Botox - there is a new idea for its application. To put it plainly, it may have to be injected in other areas not commonly associated with migraine.

It's difficult to assess the available data, as there are a great number of individual reports. A bunch of white noise that doesn't really convince me.
What exactly is smoked? How is it rolled? Where is it planted? Nobody knows. I would find its effectiveness impractical and any presumed medical potential is overblown. It's expected to help with far too many things.

Such promises of a cure-all just make me suspicious. And my lack of trust is not alleviated by the fact that many of its supporters suffer from literacy problems, to say nothing of the negative reports that are only submitted secretly because nobody wants to be outed as a consumer.
I think the topic is dry and uninteresting. The recent "legalisation" won't change that.

Next topic: the GON blockade – I have "something" injected into the back of my neck.
This is both the problem and the potential of the method. In short: it seems to be about WHAT is being injected WH Dr. Bauer from the St. Rochus Hospital in Castrop-Rauxel reports very positive results from his own clinic, but also rather wild states of the practice around the world. There is no consistency in what is being injected where. The anaesthetist's dexterity is also very crucial, and the question of, "If it didn't work, should I try it again somewhere else?" answers itself.

Personally, I have never requested such a blockade of the greater occipital nerve. But Rochus in Castrop-Rauxel is only 5 km from where I live. So you can guess what I'm going to be trying out during the next episode. A little prickling in the back of my neck. Ultrasound-guided, please.

It all reminds me of the situation facing speech pathologists. The director of the representing federal association admitted in an interview that nobody has any idea or overview of which treatments individual speech pathologists employ and how effective they even are. Everybody just does what they want.
Trying things out is good. And research should be unbiased. But in the end I like it when it all boils down to rational, evidence-based methodology. Not when something worked for somebody my neighbour's brother-in-law knows.

I will mercilessly skip over the topic "Can self-help still be saved?" and without explanation.
After the lunch break the SPG stimulator gets its spot. Everything is said about the procedure in and of itself, because it is now being extensively introduced and presented in Bochum for the third time. Because ATI sponsors the event, this is understandable, and because of the development presented I find it legitimate.
Dr. Assaf and Dr. Kohlmeier have performed 82 implants in Hamburg since 2013. In fact, with 25 operations last year, they hold the leading spot worldwide.
The procedure of the "navigated" operation presented at the last event has since become established. It takes longer, but the stimulator can be positioned more precisely. It remains uncertain whether this increases the effectiveness.
The continuously rising numbers confirm that many patients have benefited from the procedure.
I saw the word "reimplantation" on a label, and I personally know somebody with two stimulators. On both sides. If you have any special requests, these two Hamburgers are clearly happy to listen.
The manufacturer surely hopes that the stimulator will also be used for migraine. This is currently in the study phase, actually. It would possibly be the first time that migraineurs actually got something from clusterheads, and not the other way around.

The ending for me is the presentation of the results of the cornea microscopy study conducted in Bochum. It was entirely uncharted territory and a completely new idea. But research is open and unbiased, and the idea behind it could not be confirmed. Verification of the high-tech medicine on cluster headache would have been dreadfully abstracted and simplified.

After Patient Day is before Patient School. We want to hold another one in autumn, in this case the CSG NRW e.V. Probably in Düsseldorf. See you at the next "seminar".

On Accepting Lactose Intolerance
Or: To Hell with No Barriers!

Actually it all started out completely differently. That is the overarching theme of outside and self-acceptance of primary headache diseases, from migraine to cluster headache. We clusterheads tend to complain about the name of the sickness. Does it have to be called that? It's more than a headache. So is migraine. But it doesn't really help either. I pontificated on that in my book, and there have since been no changes to this acknowledgment nor to the situation as a whole. There are diseases that have a sort of shock factor. That "thank-God-I-don't-have-that" aspect. And then there's, "Oh yeah, I've had headaches before, too."
Now, that's not entirely fair.
When we talk about migraine that's about 10 % of the population. And they also have friends and relatives. Some people who take the matter seriously come together. Yet we are making no progress in the perception of Parkinson's or epilepsy.

So how did it start? Why are you writing all of this?
So that we will not be alone.
It was this tweet from Markus A. Dahlem that brought Kristina Wilms to my attention.

Visit Markus' blog for the full context: http://scilogs.spektrum.de/graue-substanz/depression/

Laut gedacht with Kristina Wilms:

Where there is now a second part there used to only be one. But the second is better:

Kristina wonderfully gets to the point on this sense of misery. Including when it comes to her depression. She says:

"Whereas I often wished I could have something proper. Something you can see or even touch."

Watched the video. Got curious. What is yet to be learned about this woman?
I admit, I like what she says and how she says it.
"I was a remaindered book," she says in an interview on Spiegel Online
http://www.spiegel.de/gesundheit/ernaehrung/selbsthilfe-app-arya-fuer-psychisch-erkrankte-a-1096751.html

There she also says, "I wanted to turn my disease and my experiences into something positive."
The peer approach. Always successfully implemented in classic self-help, but not so much in the modern age. Social media has opted for too many side-effects to provide assistance of equal quality. It's just more comfortable. Yet comfort rarely achieves goals. That's another post entirely, though.

Back to Kristina:

"I do always have my smartphone on me. It simply serves as a bridge for me to cross from therapeutic tasks back to my daily routine."

Okay - this is the moment where it becomes clear I'm from a different generation. I had been an adult for some time before smartphones came into my life, and for me they are a highly practical and valuable tool in some regards. They are not a part of my life, and they are not only used for good. I also don't share the "digital is better" mind-set when it comes to keeping headache journals. It makes sense to keep one in any case. But what's important is that you have one, not so much how you write it all down. It comes down to personal preference. Kind of like sports. You have to like doing it, and cannot be forced into it. Someone may have the urge to scribble pictures of their

mood in their journal. Then the app is useless. The means of conveying the content to a doctor have also been rather theoretical so far. Technology makes a lot of things conceivable, but there are no standards yet. Apps are an important tool - no more, but also no less.
I'll just quickly paste the link to Kristina's app here for advertising, and I'm happy to:
https://www.aryaapp.co/

If you want to take a closer look at the materials, you can read here:
https://m-sense.de/blog/2017/schmerzen-aufschreiben

For the sake of completeness, here are two links to migraine apps that I'm familiar with. They are both in German.
M-Sense: https://m-sense.de/
Migräne-App:
http://www.schmerzklinik.de/2016/10/01/die-migraene-app/

Now I'm not certain if these can present the staccato-like attack frequency typical of cluster headache. And I'm not up to date on specific cluster apps. I'm not the app guy.
But to my surprise, health insurance providers are right on the money in this regard.
http://www.abendblatt.de/nachrichten/article210264599/Studie-deutet-auf-Wirksamkeit-von-Migraene-App-hin.html
Whereby … if pure self-management leads to improvement, then the health insurance providers think that's great. And they can do that because it helps the patient, making it a win-win situation.

Those were the thoughts that marinated over a few weeks. And then there was the cherry on top.
Have you ever been to a seminar or continued education course where you spend the whole day sitting with mostly

strangers, and after a few hours of official business/formalities you get to have lunch? And was there another participant who complains about the lack of lactose-free food, even though they had the option to choose lactose-free food when they signed up?
Wow!
Just, wow!
Embarrassed silence all around. The cook comes out personally to apologise.

"In principle it's not a problem. But unfortunately I was not told anything."

The objective reason was probably so simple. The request was not conveyed from the registration to the kitchen. We are all people, after all, and we make mistakes. Thankfully! Otherwise I would not have been able to witness this acceptance.
I also was not at this educational course, and happened to be eating in the same room at the time, so I had a seat to spectate from. And I don't want to be disparaging - the woman with lactose intolerance had a very pleasant appearance and I would be happy to enjoy lactose-free ice cream with her any time.
It was this unanimous acceptance and concern that made me shoot out from my skin, and I still look back on the different "levels" of diseases. Food intolerances can also not be seen. However, they can be palpable. A definite lactose/gluten/fructose/whatever intolerance comes with a very comprehensible cause-and-effect principle. When it comes to general irritable bowel syndrome, people usually haven't taken a close enough look. There are (experimental) endoscopic methods, and journals make sense here as well. But I digress.
There is visible and invisible. Socially accepted and unaccepted. Depending on these, you will find more or less understanding people. It would be nice if the world went without air fresheners and perfumes, got rid of all

humming sounds, and made everything quieter for just one day - but I don't expect it, of course.

Getting heated up about how things should be can cost a lot more energy than simply acting more skillfully. After all, you have more influence over yourself than over other people.

From wood to branch

Sometimes I think, "I've been doing this for too long."
From working in self-help, then writing a book about it, and ultimately somehow turning the disease into a hobby. There are days when that seems strange to me. It is on those days that I think, "You have your way. You have good days and bad. You know what you have to do on the bad days. And on the good days - live!"
But that alone doesn't take me out of the woods, and on good days I always catch myself devoting my time to my not entirely voluntary hobby.
I had similar thoughts while in a cluster headache group in a large social network, where I read the assumption that cluster tends to be "left-sided". Followed by the question of whether right-sided pain feels differently than left-sided.
My immediate thought was, "Huh?"
First, the presumption of predominant left-sidedness because of some news on a social network is a rather bold hypothesis. But, sadly, it happens. Three people write in succession about the left side, and - bam - your cerebral gyri have processed "left". Insanely, it will not go away so easily.
I don't read into these networks, let alone the content. I've become careful. Because sitting on the other side are people I don't know - here I'm being heretical - and may only be claiming or believing that they have a disease like mine. It's impossible for me to test it for myself.
Left-dominant. Of course cluster isn't left-dominant - or is it?

I know lefties and I know righties. Personally. I also know people whose sides have changed. For many years. And of course it hurts just as much the other way around. A change may be confusing, as a sufferer may have gotten used to "their" side after so many years.
Strange question.
I thought so, anyway.
But a question nonetheless.
A question that has posed itself to somebody. Something that has preoccupied somebody.
It was written out and formulated. Punctuation and all, not just stammered together on a phone during a train ride. In that case I hardly would have acknowledged it.
So is cluster left-dominant or not?
It's unilateral. It is specifically defined as such, and every other sufferer I have met has described it that way. Why isn't there a bilateral manifestation of cluster, actually? That would be another question, and at its core it isn't illogical. But I've never seen it. And never been faced with it. That's simply how it is. If I'm left right now and you're right, does your right side hurt just as much as my left?
Why don't I ask myself that? Others do. So I do wonder, and actually never immediately realised it. Even worse: at first I thought it was a silly and unnecessary question.
Hence my emphatic, spontaneous reaction: "Huh?"
Why indeed. Why do others wonder, but not me.
The answer is shockingly simple: I've had enough. I'm done.
I actually don't like to talk about the manifestation of cluster headache anymore. I want to keep learning and be open to experiments and studies. See study participation here: Victim, you - study participation. But I now seem to be over all of the elementary questions for the time being. Some of them may not be particularly helpful, and others so ingrained that it's seen as a fact of life instead of a question. Perhaps like the fact that the pain is only unilateral. Why is that? I don't know, and I stopped wondering a long time ago.

So the "Huh?" turns into a silent "Ahh!"
But it's also because of a recent "grounding" in very real life, outside of cyberspace. Standing across from someone for whom the first attempts at treatment did not work so well. Plus an attending physician who only read the headings of the guidelines and nothing more.
The book and this blog are ultimately here to take away some of that person's uncertainty and to give them some hope in its place. And it's why I keep embarking on self-help days so people can take pens from me. Because there is always somebody who is doing the same as I once was.

And there are also people who simply don't learn, and who ask the same questions after months or even years. That's nothing more than exhausting. But there are also people who ask the same questions that you do simply because they are in a different spot. In this case the experienced are certainly in a position to reach out to the inexperienced.

The very last page

It's okay to fall down,
but not to stay down.

cause

Falling down is an accident.
Staying down is a choice.

So long, and thanks for all the fish.

Printed in Dunstable, United Kingdom